Intermediate

Just

For class or
self-study

Reading and Writing

Jeremy Harmer

ELT Marshall Cavendish London • Singapore • New York

The *Just* Series

The *Just* series is an integrated series of books that can be used on their own or, when used together, that make up a complete course with a consistent methodological approach. The *Just* series is designed for individual skills and language development either as part of a classroom-based course or a self-study programme. The approach is learner-centred, and each unit has clear aims, motivating topics and interesting practice activities.

The *Just* series is for adult intermediate learners and can be used as general preparation material for exams at this level.

The *Just* series has four titles:
Just Listening and Speaking 0 462 00714 6
Just Reading and Writing 0 462 00711 1
Just Grammar 0 462 00713 8
Just Vocabulary 0 462 00712 X

Marshall Cavendish ELT
119 Wardour Street
London W1F 0UW

Designed by Hart McLeod, Cambridge
Editorial development by Ocelot Publishing, Oxford
Illustrations by Yane Christiansen, Rod Hunt and Jennifer Ward

Printed and bound by Times Offset (M) Sdn. Bhd. Malaysia

Photo acknowledgements

p8 All pictures by Ronald Grant Archive; p12 Rex Features; p14 The Argus, Brighton /Richard Grange; p21 ©Royalty-Free/Corbis; p22 ©So Hing-Keung/Corbis; p23 top ©Martin Peters/ImageState/Alamy; p23 Topham Picturepoint; p24 Pictures Colour Library; p26 By permission of Penguin Books; p26 Ronald Grant Archive; p27 Ronald Grant Archive; p28 top/bottom ©Robert Harding World Imagery/Robert Harding Picture Library Ltd/Alamy; p30 Tim Heatherington/Network Photographers; p36 Bettman/Corbis; p36 Rex Features; p37 Corbis; p38 Marshall Cavendish Archive; p38 The Bridgeman Art Library, Portrait of Ann Boleyn(1507-36), Second wife of Henry VIII of England, 1534 by English School (16th century) Hever Castle Ltd, Kent, UK; p38 The Bridgeman Art Library Portrait of Catherine Howard (c.1520-d.1542) 5th Queen of Henry VIII from 'Memoirs of the Court of Queen Elizabeth', published in 1825 (w/c and gouache on paper) by Sarah Countess of Essex (d. (1838) Private Collection /The Stapleton Collection; p38 The Bridgeman Art Library Portrait of Catherine Parr (1512-48) sixth wife of Henry VIII (1491-1547) (panel) by English School (16th Century), National Portrait Gallery London UK, Roger-Viollet, Paris; p38 AKG London/Eric Lessing Jane Seymour (1509-37) p38 AKG London/Eric Lessing Anne of Cleves (1515-57); p38 AKG London Catherine of Aragon (1485-1536); p44 Topham Picturepoint; p44 Marshall Cavendish Archive; p50 Ronald Grant Archive; p50 Jean Michel Basquiat, The Horn Players, 1983 ©ADAGP, Paris and DACS, London 2003/The Broad Art Foundation; p54 a-f ©Reeve Photography; p54 d ©H, Rogers/Art Directors and Trip; p62 ©D K Khattiya/Alamy; p64 ©Reeve Photography; p66 Paul Almasy/Corbis; p66 Ronald Grant Archive; p69 By permission of Margaret Johnson/ Cambridge University Press; p70 By permission of Harper Collins Publisher; p70 By permission of Penguin Books; p70 By permission of Random House; p70 By permission of Faber and Faber for their book cover 'Kitchen' by Banana Yoshimoto; p70 Little Brown; p74 Lina Arnoff; p76 ©Reeve Photography; p78 Redferns; p80 ©Paul Lowe/ Panos Pictures; p81 by kind permission of David Wilde ©2002 Delphian Records Ltd.

Text acknowledgements

p14 based on Plane crashes into house, ©Daily Mail 02/04/01; p18 based on Shopping by John Crace, ©Guardian; p24 Backpackerland, based on an article by Jason Burke, Observer Newspapers; p26 Extract from The Beach, Alex Garland (Viking, 1996) ©Alex Garland, 1996; p30 No Home, No Job, No Worries ©C J Stone, from The Big Issue 11-17 August 1997; p32 The Confession ©Brian Patten; p33 I Am Completely Different, translation ©James Kirkup, original ©Karoda Saburo; p42 How to make those New Year's resolutions stick, ©Dr Pauline Wallin; p44 Marathon marriage just the tip of the iceberg, based Angel of the Bridge ©Daily Mail 23/04/01; p52 Neighbour bites dog in fence dispute, ©Jeremy Harmer, reprinted by permission of Pearson Education Limited; p60 Wired? Not worth it! based on Dumbing Us Down ©Theodore Rosznak, News Internationalist issue 26, December 1996; p68 Extract from All I want ©Margaret Johnson; p74 Not just a man's game, based on Something for the Ladies ©Stephanie Merritt, Observer Sports Monthly, April 2001; p84 Rachel, taken from Trumpet Voluntary, ©Jeremy Harmer; p86 Is This Love? A Closer Look, based on an article by Bob Narindra.

Contents

Introduction

For the student

Just Reading and Writing (*Intermediate*) is part of an integrated series of books designed for you to study on your own, or together with other students and a teacher. It will help you improve your reading and writing skills in English.

We have chosen the texts and tasks carefully to offer an interesting and challenging mix of topics and language styles. We have included contemporary uses of English such as email, the Internet and text messaging.

This book has a lot of practice exercises to help you with reading and writing. When you see this symbol () at the end of an exercise it means that you can refer to the Answer Key at the back of the book and check your answers there.

Although we encourage the use of dictionaries, our advice is not to use one until you have done all the exercises in a section. If you use your dictionary too early you may find it more difficult to understand the general meaning of the text.

We are confident that this book will help you progress in English and, above all, that you will enjoy using it.

For the teacher

The *Just* series is a flexible set of teaching materials that can be used on their own, or in any combination, or as a set to form a complete integrated course. The *Just* series has been written and designed using a consistent methodological approach that allows the books to be used easily together. Each book in the series specialises in either language skills or aspects of the English language. It can be used either in class or by students working on their own.

Just Reading and Writing consists of 14 units, containing a variety of reading texts and exercises on subjects such as music, graffiti, information technology, football, tourism and survival. These are designed to give students experience of reading and writing in different styles of English. There is a comprehensive Answer Key at the back of the book, and where free writing is required an 'example answer' is given.

Our aim has been to provide texts and tasks that are in themselves stimulating and that could lead to any number of different activities once the exercises in this book have been completed.

We are confident that you will find this book a real asset and that you will also want to try the other titles in the series: *Just Vocabulary*, *Just Grammar* and *Just Listening and Speaking*.

•••A Check your character

1 Read the following personality questionnaire and choose an answer for each question.

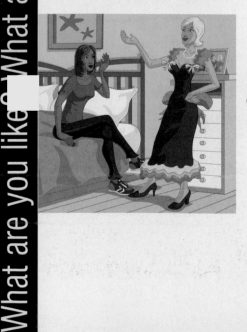

1 At the end of a romantic film when the girl and the boy finally say they love each other, do you:
a wish you'd gone to a film with lots of guns and explosions?
b feel bored?
c cry?

2 You watch a friend or relative win in a sports competition. Do you:
a clap politely but happily?
b clap enthusiastically, and encourage other people to do the same?
c jump up and down, cheering as loudly as you can?

3 It's Friday evening. You've had a long and tiring week. Do you:
a stay at home and read a book?
b go to a show or film with a friend?
c go to a club with a group of friends?

4 Someone wants to talk to you about their problems while you are watching a TV programme. Do you:
a say 'Not now, I'm watching television'?
b continue to watch television while they talk?
c turn off the television and listen attentively?

5 Your brother's friend rings to say that he's just arrived in your town, but you already have plans to go out with another friend. Do you:
a say 'How lovely to hear from you. What a pity I'm just going out'?
b try and find out how long he's going to stay before asking him over?
c invite him to your house straight away?

6 A friend criticises something new you are wearing. Do you:
a say 'I don't care what you think. I like it'?
b decide never to wear it again?
c go home and change immediately?

7 Someone asks you to give them a lift in your car, but they want to go somewhere different from you. Do you:
a say 'I'm sorry, I don't want to go that way'?
b say 'Yes, but I wasn't going to go that way'?
c say 'Yes of course', even though it's inconvenient?

8 At work, your boss asks you if you can work at the weekend to finish an urgent job. Do you:
a refuse politely and say 'The weekend is for my family'?
b say 'I'm not sure. I need to think about it'?
c agree immediately because you want to be helpful?

9 You don't feel like going to work or school because you went to a party last night. Do you:
a call and say 'My friend isn't feeling very well. I'm staying at home to look after him'?
b call and say you are ill?
c go into work or school and try your best?

10 Someone falls off their bicycle in the street in front of you. Do you:
a call out 'Are you OK?' but keep on walking?
b run to get help?
c keep walking because you have an important appointment and you don't want to be late?

2 Check your answers with the questionnaire key (shown at the bottom of the page). Write the words that describe you.

....

....

3 Find the words in the questionnaire with the following meanings. (The first letter of each word is given.) The first answer is done for you.

a Someone who is linked to you by marriage or blood is a r.*elative*........................... .

b If you do something with a lot of energy and passion you do it e................................ .

c If you listen, read or watch very carefully, you do it a................................ .

d If you say something bad about someone or something you c........................... them/it.

e Something that is not helpful because it wastes your time is i............................... .

f If you do something to the best of your ability you t............ y............ b............ .

4 Look again at the questionnaire. Write three more questions about the situations below. Use the questions in the questionnaire as models (give three alternatives, a, b and c) for each situation. If you can, find someone else to answer them.

1 You see a child crying at a bus stop. Do you:

a ....

b ....

c ....

2 Two people are arguing loudly in a restaurant where you are having dinner. Do you:

a ....

b ....

c ....

3 Your grandfather has given you a special book. Your friend asks to borrow it. Do you:

a ....

b ....

c ....

QUESTIONNAIRE KEY

Find out what your answers mean.

If you answered mostly a: you are often assertive, decisive, strong and sincere. You are a good leader and the perfect person to follow in an emergency.

If you answered mostly b: you are often considerate, friendly, patient and honest. People trust you and they are right to do so.

If you answered mostly c: you are often emotional, kind, romantic and sympathetic. People turn to you when they have problems. You like to be with others and they like to be with you.

If you chose different letters each time you must have all of these characteristics and are therefore probably perfect!

•••B The story of Eugene Onegin

1 Read the story of Eugene Onegin (below) and then put the pictures (a–f) in the right order (1–6).

1 ....   2 ....   3 ....   4 ....   5 ....   6 ....

One of the greatest works of Russian literature is the poem *Eugene Onegin* by Aleksandr Pushkin (1799–1837). Ever since its publication in 1825 it has remained popular. It was made into an opera by the Russian composer Tchaikovsky and, a few years ago, into a film starring the British actor Ralph Fiennes.

The story of Eugene Onegin tells of Madam Larina, a widow, who lives in the country with her two daughters, Olga and Tatiana. Olga is more cheerful and outgoing than her younger sister, who spends her time reading romantic novels. Olga is engaged to the young landowner, Lensky.

One day Lensky brings a friend from the city (St Petersburg) to visit Madam Larina and her daughters. He is Eugene Onegin, a man who has decided to be cynical, unemotional and bored by life. Tatiana doesn't realise this and falls passionately in love with him almost the moment she sees him. She writes a letter to tell him so, pouring out her adolescent heart, sure that he will answer her. But Onegin does not love Tatiana, of course. At least he does not love 'love', and so he tells her not to be so ridiculous. Tatiana is heartbroken.

A few days later Madam Larina throws a big party for Tatiana's birthday. People come from all the estates near hers, and there is much dancing and singing. Onegin is there too, but he is in a strange mood and, for his own amusement, he starts flirting with Olga. He jokes with her and dances with her, so that Lensky is first jealous and then absolutely furious. He challenges Onegin to a duel.

The next morning, early, while the mist still hangs over the lake near Madam Larina's house, the two men meet. They both know that fighting each other is stupid, but they can't stop what is about to happen. They take out their pistols. Onegin fires first and Lensky, his friend, falls to the ground. Onegin has killed him and so he has no choice but to leave – and quickly. He goes to live abroad, away from Russia.

Three years later he returns to St Petersburg. Enough time has passed, he thinks, for people to have forgotten about Lensky's death. On his first night back home he goes to a big ball. All of St Petersburg society is there.

Onegin sees a beautiful young girl dancing with her elderly husband, Prince Gremin. He can hardly take his eyes off her and realises, suddenly, that it is Tatiana; he realises, too, that he loves her – that he has always loved her. In an ironic twist of fate he now writes her his own letter pouring out his love for her. She agrees to meet him, and he begs her to leave her husband to be with him.

Tatiana is torn between her feelings for Onegin (whom she still loves) and her duty to Prince Gremin (who is kind to her and to whom, after all, she is married). She is angry with Onegin. Why has it taken him so long to realise how he feels about her? If only, if only. She tells him he has come too late, that however much she wants to she can not walk away from her marriage. This time it is Eugene Onegin who leaves the meeting with a broken heart, to walk the streets of St Petersburg in misery.

In a final twist of fate, in 1837, the writer of the poem, Pushkin, was himself killed in a duel – just like Lensky, the character in the story.

2 Answer the following questions. The first one is done for you.

a Who challenges Onegin to a duel? ....Lensky.......................

b Who falls in love with Onegin? ....

c Who has a fiancée called Olga? ....

d Who has two daughters? ....

e Who kills Lensky? ....

f Who starred in a film of *Eugene Onegin*? ....

g Who married Tatiana? ....

h Who asks Tatiana to leave her husband? ....

i Who writes letters? ....

j Who wrote the opera *Eugene Onegin*? ....

k Who wrote the poem *Eugene Onegin*? ....

l Who was killed in 1837? ....

3 Look at the way the words in the box are used in the story of Eugene Onegin and then write them in the sentences. The first one is done for you.

a twist of fate
can not walk away from
challenges someone to a duel
fictional
heartbroken
in a strange mood
landowner
outgoing
passionately
pours out their heart
ridiculous
widow

a If someone is a ......widow....... it means her husband has died.

b If someone .... it means they tell you honestly and passionately how they feel.

c If someone .... it means they are asking someone to fight them, perhaps to the death.

d If someone .... something it means they can not abandon it.

e If someone is .... it means they feel different from usual and other people notice this.

f If someone is .... in love it means they are very much in love.

g If someone is .... it means they talk a lot, are friendly and enjoy meeting people.

h If someone is .... it means someone they love has left them or died and they are very sad.

i If someone is a .... it means they have some land.

j If someone is a .... character it means they do not really exist, but they are in a story, film or play.

k If something is .... it means it is silly, not sensible.

l We call it .... when a strange, unexpected thing happens.

●●●C Personal reports

1 Miss Smith, the history teacher, wrote these reports about her students.

In spite of his enthusiastic and friendly nature, Justin is often far too emotional. His romantic ideas often amuse the rest of the class and he gets very upset because of their behaviour. This is a pity because he is intelligent and often shows initiative.

Despite her intelligence, Sally is extremely assertive and rather inconsiderate to other members of the class. She is often impatient with her classmates and unsympathetic to their difficulties.

Although John tries his best, he is just not very intelligent. He does not seem able to show initiative, and because he is not very decisive he is not making much progress.

The head of the college has asked Miss Smith to write the reports again (see a–c below), but this time to be completely positive. Which student is she writing about in each one?

a .... is a decisive and intelligent worker, shows considerable initiative and is very enthusiastic.

b .... is conscientious, friendly and pleasant, and a pleasure to have in the class with us.

c .... is a happy, sensitive student, obviously sincere, and a loyal classmate. Contributions to class discussion from this student are always interesting.

2 Look at how the different linking words in the reports are followed by different grammatical patterns.

LINKING WORDS

● The words *although* and *because* are followed by a clause containing a *subject* and a *verb*:
Although John tries his best …
● … *because* he is not very decisive …

● *In spite of*, *despite* and *because of* are followed by a *noun* or *-ing form verb*:
In spite of his enthusiastic and friendly nature …
Despite her intelligence …
… *because of* their behaviour …

3 Now combine phrases and sentences from Box A with phrases and sentences from Box C using one of the linking words in Box B. Write your answers in the spaces below (one is done for you).

A	B	C
He is happy	although	getting up early.
Stephen is very excited		he has just won the lottery.
He played a good game	in spite of	he is not very big.
She missed the train		she is not very intelligent.
Arran is a good football player	because	his lottery win.
Mark is not very popular		his hard work.
He failed his exam	despite	his friendly and enthusiastic manner.
Sadia passed her exam		feeling ill.
	because of	

He is happy because he has just won the lottery.

....

....

....

....

....

....

....

4 Write two reports about Andrew Tregarron using the appropriate information given in the box below. In the first report you should be honest, and in the second more positive. Follow the patterns you have looked at in Exercises 1–3 above.

Report 1

....

....

....

....

....

Report 2

....

....

....

....

....

a fast worker

makes mistakes

not very popular (tries too hard to make friends)

obsessed with music

sometimes careless

tries his best to make friends

very creative

very musical

•••A Overalls

1 Read the newspaper report below and then answer these questions.

a What saved someone? ....

b Who was saved? ....

c What was he saved from? ....

OVERALLS SAVE ABANDONED SAILOR

by Washington correspondent Anthony Dorking

A young US marine survived for nearly two days alone in the Arabian Sea, thanks to a pair of regulation overalls, according to the latest press release from the Pentagon.

Lt Zachary Mayo, a 20-year-old lance corporal in the US Navy, woke up and couldn't get back to sleep. His cabin was too hot and stuffy. He got off his bunk quietly so as not to wake his shipmates. He put his blue overalls over his shorts and T-shirt he had been sleeping in, and left the cabin.

Zachary Mayo went up onto the deck of the USS America, a huge aircraft carrier. It was two o'clock on a Friday morning. He breathed in the fresh air and looked up at the stars in the clear night sky. And then, without thinking, he leaned out too far and lost his footing. Before he knew it, he was in the water, watching the huge ship disappearing into the night. Nobody had seen him fall, and for nearly two days not one of the 4,700 crew realised he had gone.

Mayo survived because at training camp two years before, he had been taught how to make clothes into life jackets. He took off his overalls and tied the arms and legs. Then he waved his 'life jacket' over his head and filled it with air so he could stay afloat. He did this many times during his ordeal.

After 34 hours, Mayo was sure he would die. He hadn't seen any search planes, and twice he had seen sharks swimming around him. Both nights that he was in the water he was attacked by smaller fish and he was slowly dying of thirst.

Finally he fell asleep. When he woke up his overalls were floating away from him. In a fit of madness he tore off his T-shirt and shorts and prepared to die. And then, half an hour later, just before he lost consciousness, he saw a small boat.

A Pakistani fisherman, Abdul Aziz, was out in his boat that day. He couldn't believe his eyes when he saw Mayo's naked body, floating in the Arabian Sea, 100 miles from land. 'I thought it was a ghost!' he told reporters. But it was not a ghost. It was Zachary Mayo, and he was alive! But only just.

Two marines had been to see Mayo's parents in Osburn, Idaho, USA, to say that he was missing. His parents were desperately hoping for a miracle but they were almost sure that he was dead. They had to wait three days for news of his incredible rescue.

2 Read the text again and answer the following questions in your own words.

a Why did Mayo go onto the deck?

....

....

....

b How did he fall into the sea?

....

....

....

c How did his overalls help him to survive?

....

....

....

d Why did he think he was going to die?

....

....

....

e Who talked to Lt Mayo's parents, and what happened three days later?

....

....

....

3 Find words or phrases in the text with the following meanings.

a publicity and/or news given by an official organisation:...

b the headquarters of the armed forces in the United States of America:.........................

c airless, a feeling that it is difficult to breathe:

....

d a small bed often built above or below another bed, found in ships and in children's bedrooms:

....

e the surface that you walk on, on a ship:

....

f a ship that planes can land on and take off from:...

g a terrible experience:

....

h a fantastic and amazing event:

....

Language in chunks

4 Read the definitions and then complete the following phrases from the text.

a to go to sleep again

He couldn't get ....

b he didn't think

Without ....

c to be unable to stand up, suddenly

[Mayo] lost his ....

d to behave in a crazy way for a moment

In a fit ....

e to stop being aware of the world

just before he lost ....

f to see something you can't believe

Abdul Aziz couldn't believe ....

B Not a very ordinary day

1 Read the newspaper article below and then complete the table.

	Name(s)	Occupation(s)
People who live in the house:		
Pilot:		

My amazing escape

(from *The Daily Mail*)

When Helen Monahan got a phone call asking her to pick up a friend's children from school while collecting her own she grabbed her coat and headed down the road.

It meant leaving home five minutes earlier than she had intended – but it could also have saved her life.

Minutes after she shut the door, a light aircraft crashed on to her empty house.

'I am trying not to think what would have happened if I had left home at the normal time,' said Mrs Monahan.

Pilot Donald Campbell also had reason to be thankful. The 52-year-old neurosurgeon walked away from the wreckage with only minor injuries to his face and head.

He had been steering the four-seater Piper Seneca towards Shoreham Airport in West Sussex when the twin engines cut out.

It plunged and clipped a railway bridge, before ploughing through the roof of the £150,000 three-bedroom house in the town of Shoreham-by-Sea.

It toppled into the back garden, which was strewn with children's toys.

Mrs Monahan, 36, said: 'It looks like something out of a film set. The tail of the plane was up in the air and the nose was in the fish pond.' Her husband Marcus, a 33-year-old boiler engineer, was at work at the time of the crash, and their children – Harley, six, and five-year-old Norton – were in school.

Mr Campbell, who flies all over the country to treat the patients of his private practice, said: 'I was coming into the airport and both engines cut out. It began to yaw quite sharply to one side.

'I couldn't land on the railway line because of the electric cable and I saw a gap by the houses and aimed next to them.

'I remember a bang. The port wing tip must have hit the roof. It was a bit rough.'

Safety officials were last night examining the plane to try to discover what went wrong.

2 Is each of the following statements *True* or *False*? Write T or F in the brackets.

   a Mrs Monahan collected two children from school on the   [   ]
      day of the crash.
   b Nobody was seriously hurt in the crash.   [   ]
   c The pilot knows why the engines stopped suddenly.   [   ]
   d The pilot tried to land on the railway line.   [   ]
   e The pilot flies a lot.   [   ]
   f There were children's toys in the garden before the   [   ]
      aeroplane landed there.
   g The first thing that the plane hit was the roof.   [   ] ☞

3 Look at the way the verbs in the box are used in the newspaper report and then write each one next to the correct dictionary definition below. (The first one is done for you.)

   a to collect someone who is waiting for you: ....*pick up*.............

   b to control the direction of a vehicle or aircraft: ....

   c to fall or move down very quickly and with force: ....

   d to get something quickly because you do not have much time:

      ....

   e to give medical care to someone: ....

   f to hit something quickly and lightly: ....

   g to hit something with great force and then continue moving:

      ....

   h to move away from its proper course: ....

   i to suddenly stop working: .... ☞

clip
cut out
grab
pick up
plough through
plunge
steer
treat
yaw

4 Look at this diagram of a Piper Seneca aeroplane. Label it with as many words from the text as you can.

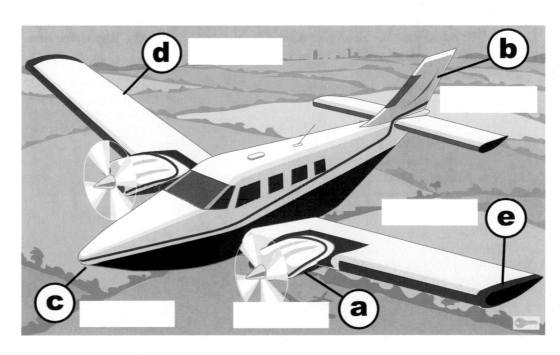

•• C Headlines and newspapers

1 Match phrases from the two columns below to make newspaper headlines.

a Fuel ....

b Hero ....

c Horrified ....

d Saved ....

e Turbulence ....

Fuel gauge	**sees attack**
Hero pulls	**terrifies teenager**
Horrified driver	**sharp-eyed flight attendant**
Saved by	**neighbour from fire**
Turbulence	**failure traps couple**

2 Look at the headlines you have made and answer the following questions.

a Which kinds of word are commonly left out?

....

b Which kinds of words are included?

....

c What happens to the tense of the verbs?

....

3 Match the following stories with the headlines from Exercise 1.

a ....

A teenager flying from Istanbul to New York was absolutely terrified when the plane she was travelling in encountered major turbulence over the Atlantic.

'We'd just had our meal when the pilot warned us about the weather,' said 16-year-old Gulay Menguç …

b ....

A horrified car owner watched as youths attacked his car with bricks and a baseball bat.

'I had just come out of the house, when I saw this gang of youths. They were throwing things at my car and hitting it with a baseball bat …'

c ....

How good is your eyesight? Could you see a burning ship from 35,000 feet? That's just what Julie did and today we say 'She's a hero!'

Julie was working on a flight between Taipei and Sydney when she looked out of the window …

d ....

A courageous villager battled through a burning bungalow to carry his neighbour to safety.

Hero Laurence Broderick rescued Jean Buiter after a fire tore through her home in High Street, Waresly, destroying much of the roof.

e ....

A frightened couple spent the night in their car in freezing temperatures after they ran out of fuel.

'The gauge said we still had half a tank of petrol,' said Jane Bakewell after their ordeal, 'but then the car suddenly stopped and I had forgotten to bring my mobile phone with me, so …'

4 Answer the following questions.

a Who was terrified where, after what?

....

b Who attacked what with what?

....

c Who saw what, from where?

....

d Who was saved from what, by who, where?

....

e Who had forgotten what, and what effect did it have?

....

5 Write headlines to go at the beginning of these newspaper articles.

a ....

A worker at Simpsons, the California meat packing company, was locked in a freezer cabinet all night when the door was closed while he was inside. 'It was so cold I nearly died,' he said, 'but I ran around all night and that kept me warm ...'

b ....

Two people were killed on Thursday when a large lorry crossed over the central section of the M40 motorway and smashed into a car. Police are investigating the incident.

c ....

Fans of the band Warmheart were disappointed last night when their concert was cancelled. They were given tickets for the next concert tour in June.

'We were very sorry,' said Warmheart's manager, 'but two of the band members, Ronnie and Chris, were very unwell. They just couldn't play. I nearly sent them to hospital.'

d ....

A brave young girl is running a special marathon race in Bangkok tomorrow to raise money for cancer research.

'My mother had cancer,' said Emma. 'She's better now, but I wanted to do something for people in the future.'

Emma, who is 15 years old, has been training for two weeks. 'I'm nervous about the race,' she said. 'It's very long. But I'm going to raise a lot of money from my sponsors.'

6 Using any words from this unit, write a newspaper headline. Then write a short newspaper article to go with it.

....
....
....
....
....

●●● A Supermarkets

1 On the supermarket plan choose the best place for:

- ...the products you want to sell most
- ...drinks
- ...the meat and fish counter
- ...fruit and vegetables

Write in the names of the products where you think they should be.

Think about what sort of colours, smells, lighting and noises there might be in the supermarket. Make a note of your ideas below.

- smells: ....
- colours: ....
- lighting: ....
- noises: ....

EXIT

ENTRANCE

2 Read the text below. Is your supermarket plan similar to this?

Few shoppers go to the supermarket with lists, so supermarkets want to encourage them to buy a lot of **everything**. How do they do this?

○ The entrance is normally at one side and the exit at the other so that shoppers walk down all the aisles before leaving.

○ Fruit and vegetables are normally close to the entrance. This makes people think they are going into an open-air market and makes them feel positive.

○ Meat and fish counters are usually placed on the back wall. Supermarkets do not want to risk putting off their customers by taking meat carcasses through the shop.

○ Some shelf spaces are better than others! The middle shelves on the left are considered the best place. Suppliers sometimes pay supermarkets for the best places!

○ Vacuum-packed meats and fish look clean and bloodless. When you buy your lamb chops you are thinking of convenience and availability rather than a lamb in the field.

○ Stores are usually decorated in colours that make people feel healthy and happy. All the supermarkets belonging to one company have the same colours to make people feel at home.

○ A person blinks an average of 32 times a minute. US research has shown that a certain type of lighting can reduce this to 14 times a minute. This can make customers feel sleepy, and they then buy more goods.

○ Goods placed at the end of an aisle often sell five times more than those placed in the middle of the aisle. Stores often move goods that they particularly want to sell, such as those nearing their sell-by date, to these sites.

○ Supermarkets try to control smells. Unpleasant aromas, such as those of fish, are taken away by air extractors. Fresh smells, such as baking bread, may be pumped around the store to create a nice 'homely' feel.

○ Most shoppers buy bread, so the bakery counter is situated as far away from the entrance as possible. Customers will have to walk past hundreds of other products to reach it.

○ Drinks are usually located near the exit. Supermarkets hope that customers will buy because they are in a good mood as they finish their shopping experience.

○ Silence makes shoppers feel uncomfortable. Supermarkets like to make sure that there is quite a lot of pleasant background noise, such as music or the hum of freezers.

○ Security cameras are not just for catching shoplifters. Supermarkets also follow a few shoppers through the shop so that they can observe what routes people take. This information helps them to rearrange their products so that people buy more.

3 Are the following facts *True* or *False* – T or F – according to the text? Give reasons for your choice.

a People go to supermarkets with a clear idea of what they are going to buy.
   T / F...

b Shoppers like the sight of fresh fruit and vegetables.
   T / F...

c Meat counters are usually near the front of a supermarket.
   T / F...

d The goods on the top shelves always sell the best.
   T / F...

e Supermarkets still don't know what colours relax people.
   T / F...

f Sleepy people buy less than people who are awake.
   T / F...

g People are influenced by what they can smell.
   T / F...

h Shoppers like silence.
   T / F...

4 Find words in the text with the following meanings. The first letter of each word is given.

a passageway between two rows of shelves: a.................................

b outside: o................-a................

c the remains of dead animals: c.................................

d in a see-through container with the air removed: v.........................-p.................

e to open and shut your eyes very quickly: b.................................

f the last day on which you can buy something: s.........................-b................ d................

g a continuous sound which is not very loud: b................................. n................

h watch: o.................................

Language in chunks

5 In the text opposite find at least four examples of the phrase *make* (*someone*) *feel* (*something*). Note them down below.

   ....

   ....

6 Which of these sentences summarise the text best?

a Supermarkets try to trick customers into buying products that they don't want. This is a bad thing.

b Supermarkets try to make shopping pleasant for their customers. This is a good thing.

●●● B Shopping and the Internet

internet.com   printer version | email this article | send feedback

What Do Online Shoppers Want?
››› The Leading Edge

When real life collides with Net life, it can really put things into perspective.

In Baltimore, Maryland we have just got a new shopping mall, and it's huge! The $250 million Arundel Mills Mall is one of the biggest shopping complexes in the United States. It has a movie theatre with more than twenty screens, there are enormous entertainment areas – and more than 7,000 parking spaces.

During its opening weekend two weeks ago, the place was a madhouse, with huge traffic queues on the exit ramps leading to the mall that extended for miles as tens of thousands of cars tried to get into too few parking spaces. Police patrolled the highways to keep shoppers from parking up to ten miles away on the side of the road and walking to the mall.

And since that opening weekend people haven't just come to look. They're buying, too. They've already spent several million dollars, and this is just the beginning of the Christmas shopping season. And every day there are stories about it on the TV or in the local papers. It's a huge success.

Shopping on the Internet isn't a success like that. True it's growing, but very slowly. People still seem to prefer the real offline experience to buying things from the comfort of their own home.

But why? Why do so many people spend so much money offline while the online sector is still creeping along? When I drove by the lines of cars going to my friendly neighborhood megamall, I thought long and hard about this question. Those people sitting in their cars (some for more than an hour!) clearly weren't there for convenience. They weren't there because they expected exceptional customer service. Sure, many of them were there because this monster was new and different and something to gawk at, but many of them were spending money.

As I drove by, all I kept asking myself was "When was the last time anybody got this excited about a new e-commerce site? Is shopping online somehow fundamentally different than shopping offline?"

I've begun to think it is, especially now that studies are showing us how and why people use (and don't use) the Internet to shop. For example one recent report shows that people only start buying on the web when they've been Internet users for some time. So people in Sweden (who've had the Internet for quite a few years) buy more than people from France (who haven't had the Internet for as long). You have to feel comfortable before you shop online!

The most successful shopping sites on the Internet are small – the ones that only offer one thing. They're quick, easy to use, don't ask for too much personal information (something that stops many people from shopping on the Internet), and don't go wrong in the middle of a shopping session. I think I now understand what it's all about. As my recent megamall experience proved to me, people in the real world are a lot more willing to put up with a lot of hassles in order to be immersed in an experience that may have shopping at its core, but also includes social and entertainment aspects. Online, it's a different story. In the end, sites that concentrate on the basics of customer focus, relevance, support, service, fulfilment, and function are the ones that are going to win... not the ones that try to fight the megamalls.

SUBSCRIBE

Email Marketing

Technology

Advertising

Customer Care

Contact Us

Archives

Email Marketing

The Leading Edge

Brand Marketing

Media Buying

Site Design

Writing Online

Ecommerce Marketing

1 Read the extract from the website opposite and then circle the best answers.

a The Arundel Mills Mall:
1 ... is a new American online Internet site.
2 ... is a new shopping centre in the United States.
3 ... is a new hospital for people with mental problems.

b The article says that Internet shopping sites are most successful when:
1 ... they try to be like the kind of shopping people do in huge megamall shopping centres.
2 ... the customers are new Internet users.
3 ... they are small and efficient and don't try to be like megamalls.

c People who go to the megamall:
1 ... go because it is convenient and the staff are extremely efficient.
2 ... go because police patrol the highways.
3 ... go for an 'experience' which includes shopping and entertainment.

d People from Sweden buy more on the Internet than people from France because:
1 ... the Internet has been in Sweden longer than it has been in France.
2 ... the Internet hasn't been in Sweden as long as it has been in France.
3 ... Swedish Internet sites are very small.

2 Match these words from the text with their definitions. The first one is done for you.

collide

convenience

creep along

efficient

exit ramps

hassle

madhouse

online

patrol

put things into perspective

queue

season

shopping offline

site

a a 'place' you visit when you use your computer to connect to the Internet: ....site..........

b a line of people or things waiting to go somewhere: ....

c a period of the year when a particular thing happens: ....

d a place where there is a lot of confusing noise and activity:
....

e short roads that are used to drive off larger main roads:
....

f connected to an Internet site: ....

g something that is annoying because it is difficult or chaotic:
....

h to bump into: ....

i to look around to make sure things are all right in an area or building: ....

j to move somewhere very slowly: ....

k something which helps you to understand how important or unimportant something is: ....

l when something is easy to use and useful for what you need:
....

m when you go shopping in the real world: ....

n working well – without wasting time or effort: ....

3 Complete the tables below with notes about (a) the megamall, and (b) online shopping sites.

a The megamall

1 Name of the mall:	
2 Cost:	
3 Location:	
4 Number of parking spaces:	
5 What's in it:	
6 Longest queues on the opening weekend:	

b Online shopping sites

1 People most likely to shop online:	
2 Qualities of good online sites:	
3 What online sites need if they are going to win:	

•• C Paragraph construction

1 Read the paragraph. What information is given about:

a ... some people? ....

b ... a lot of things? ....

c ... the majority of people? ....

d ... many people? ....

> **1** [   ] Some people think that the Internet has changed the way that people in rich countries shop. **2** [   ] It is certainly possible to buy a lot of things now – from groceries to books – without leaving the house. **3** [   ] But other commentators think that the majority of people would still rather go to a shop or supermarket with real people in it than log on to a website. **4** [   ] There is no doubt, however, that computers have had an impact on the shopping habits of many people.

2 Think about the structure of a paragraph like the one above. It is often made up of the following types of sentence:

a an introductory sentence
b an example or explanation sentence
c an exception or question sentence
d a conclusion

What type of sentence (a–d in the list above):

1 ... closes the paragraph? ....

2 ... contrasts with the introductory sentence? ....

3 ... follows on from the introductory sentence, expanding on the information in it? ....

4 ... introduces the subject matter of the paragraph? ....

3 Can you identify the different types of sentence in the paragraph in Exercise 1? Write the letter of the type of sentence in the boxes in the text.

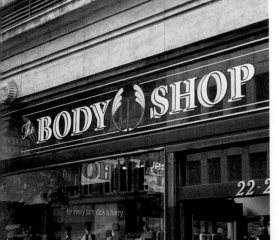

4 Put the following sentences in order to make a paragraph.

a Despite criticism, however, the shops continue to be successful in Europe and the USA, and Anita Roddick goes on working with people all over the world.

b It was founded by Anita Roddick, who wanted to sell beauty products which had not been tested on animals.

c One of the most popular organisations in Britain is The Body Shop.

d Some people do not like her claim that The Body Shop is a better kind of business because it works directly with people in developing countries.

●●● A Backpacking

1 Read the report on 'Backpackerland'. Which of the following statements best sums it up?

a Backpackerland is in Australia.
b Backpackerland is a name for any place where a certain kind of traveller goes.
c Backpackerland is the name of a kind of clothing.
d Backpackerland is a type of cybercafé.

BACKPACKERLAND

Peter Hedley on the modern way to travel – for some!

Once you've left the airport you find yourself a cheap hostel and sleep badly because it's hot, much hotter than it was when you left home, and you haven't paid enough for an air-conditioned room. Besides, there's the noise of the busy street and some crazy tourist playing a harmonica all night. On top of that you're jet-lagged because you've crossed two time zones at least. All your worst nightmares have come true, but you don't care, because this is an adventure and you aren't at home any more.

In the morning you feel exhausted but more alive than you have for years. You go out on to the street and have your first cup of coffee. Everywhere there are foreign vehicles, strange smells, different colours and people wearing different clothes. As you look up and down the street you see more and more people just like yourself, travellers – but they've been here for at least three days. They're much more interesting-looking than you, and seem completely at home as they visit the shops and market stalls, or hurry into the cybercafés to see if their mums have sent them an email. Welcome to Backpackerland.

Backpackerland is a new world of possibility, not quite real. You go into it as a third-year economics student from Liverpool, a young lawyer from Seattle, a secretary from Melbourne or a student teacher from Turin. A few dollars later you are a cross between a 19th-century adventurer, a 20th-century clubber and a 21st-century philosopher reading travel guides and writing poetry by the roadside.

Backpackerland has recognised meeting points like Khao San Road in Bangkok, the Kings Cross area of Sydney, and the Colaba Causeway in India. It exists because travel is cheaper than ever before. Each year, more and more young people cross the world from east to west, from north to south, stuffing clothes, notebooks and cameras into their backpacks to experience the clamour of Mexico City, the heat of the Atacama desert or the snowy altitudes of Nepal.

Travelling has changed out of all recognition in the last 30 years. In the old days you waited for months for a letter from your granny and if you ever did manage to phone home it cost the earth and you couldn't hear each other properly. It was only the bravest who risked cutting themselves off like that. Now you're almost never out of touch. The cybercafé computers in Kathmandu, Phnom Penh and La Paz are as fast as anything you'll find in Tokyo, Washington or Berlin. So the moment you get off the plane you can email the friend you had a drink with the day before you left home.

When I was last in Thailand I bumped into Colin, the man who'd done the electric wiring in my little flat in London. Back home he'd always seemed miserable and cold, but now Colin (who had just been exploring in the jungle) was tanned and fit, and he was smiling a lot. That's the kind of thing that happens in Backpackerland. You can be anyone you want to be and life is full of surprises.

2 Read the text again and answer the following questions.

a How old are most backpackers?.................................

b What occupations do backpackers have?

....

c Are they rich or poor?...

d Why does Backpackerland exist now?

....

e How can holidaymakers communicate with each other and with people at home when they are travelling? ....

3 Find words or phrases in the text with the following meanings.

a a small cheap hotel (paragraph 1): ....

....

b mechanically cooled (paragraph 1):.........................

....

c tired because you've travelled across the world on a plane (paragraph 1): ....

....

d places with computers which anyone can pay to use (paragraph 2): ....

e places where you can buy things – the places are often smaller than a shop, and usually in the open air (paragraph 2):.........................

....

f books specially for travellers (paragraph 3):...........

....

g noise and bustle (paragraph 4):.........................

....

h people with the most courage (paragraph 5):........

4 How many examples of comparative and superlative adjectives can you find in the text? (You should find six.)

1 ....   2 ....   3 ....

4 ....   5 ....   6 ....

Now write one of these comparative or superlative adjectives in the gap in each of the following sentences.

a Peter was .... dancer I've ever seen!

b Swimming makes you feel .... than lying in the sun.

c Juan was the .... bull fighter in Spain.

d Australia is .... than Britain.

e The novel is .... than the text book.

f Markets are usually .... than shops.

Language in chunks

5 Complete each blank with words from the box to make phrases from the text.

| at home   between (X and Y)   of surprises   of touch   the earth |

a a cross ....

b completely ....

c cost ....

d life is full ....

e out ....

B The Beach

1 Read the extract from *The Beach* that follows. Are the following sentences *True* or *False*? Write T or F in the brackets.

a The writer was woken up by his alarm clock.   [   ]
b The water pipes made a lot of noise when the writer had a bath.   [   ]
c The conversations of the people who worked in the guesthouse were easy to understand.   [   ]
d The two German girls were just setting off on their travels at five-thirty.   [   ]
e The writer started to feel hungry.   [   ]
f Breakfast was served below the writer's room.   [   ]
g The writer saw someone who he had seen in the eating area the night before.   [   ]
h The writer ordered a banana pancake and a Coca-Cola.   [   ]
i It was a sunny day.   [   ]
j A girl offered the writer a pineapple while he listened to a tape.   [   ]

This extract is from the best-selling novel *The Beach* by Alex Garland, which tells the story of a traveller in Backpackerland who starts his journey in Khao San Road.

'Has all the makings of a cult classic'
– Nick Hornby

The Beach
ALEX GARLAND

The Khao San Road woke early. At five, muffled car horns began sounding off in the street outside, Bangkok's version of the dawn chorus. Then the water pipes under the floor started to rattle as the guest-house staff took their showers. I could hear their conversations, the plaintive sound of Thai rising above the splashing water.

Lying on my bed, listening to the morning noises, the tension of the previous night became unreal and distant. Although I couldn't understand what the staff were saying to each other, their chattering and occasional laughter conveyed a sense of normality: they were doing what they did every morning, their thoughts connected only to routine. I imagined they might be discussing who would go for kitchen supplies in the market that day or who would be sweeping the halls.

Around five-thirty a few bedroom-door bolts clicked open as the early-bird travellers emerged and the die-hard party goers from Patpong returned. Two German girls clattered up the wooden stairs at the far end of my corridor, apparently wearing clogs. I realised that the dreamless snatches of sleep I'd managed were finished, so I decided to have a cigarette, the one I'd denied myself a few hours before.

The early morning smoke was a tonic. I gazed upwards, an empty matchbox for an ashtray balanced on my stomach, and every puff I blew into the ceiling lifted my spirits a little higher. Before long my mind turned to thoughts of food. I left my room to see if there was any breakfast to be had in the eating area downstairs.

There were already a few travellers at the tables, dozily sipping glasses of black coffee. One of them, still sitting on the same chair as yesterday evening was the helpful mute/heroin addict. He'd been there all night, judging from his glazed stare. As I sat down I gave him a friendly smile and he tilted his head in reply.

I began studying the menu, a once white sheet of A4 paper with such an excessive list of dishes I felt making a choice was beyond my ability. Then I was distracted by a delicious smell. A kitchen boy had wandered over with a tray of fruit pancakes. He distributed them to a group of Americans, cutting off a good-natured argument about train times to Ciang Mai.

One of them noticed me eyeing their food and he pointed at his plate. 'Banana pancakes,' he said. 'The business.'

I nodded. 'They smell pretty good.'

'Taste better. English?'

'Uh-huh.'

'Been here long?'

Since yesterday evening. You?'

'A week,' he replied, and popped a piece of pancake in his mouth, looking away as he did so. I guessed that signalled the end of the exchange.

The kitchen boy came over to my table and stood there, gazing at me expectantly through sleepy eyes.

'One banana pancake, please,' I said, obliged into making a snap decision.

'You wan' order one banan' pancake?'

'Please.'

'You wan' order drink?'

'Uh, a Coke. No, a Sprite.'

'You wan' one banan' pancake, one Spri.'

'Please.'

He strolled back towards the kitchen, and a sudden swell of happiness washed over me. The sun was bright on the road outside. A man was setting up his stall on the pavement, arranging bootleg tapes into rows. Next to him a small girl sliced pineapples, cutting the tough skin into neat, spiralling designs. Behind her an even smaller girl used a rag to keep the flies at bay.

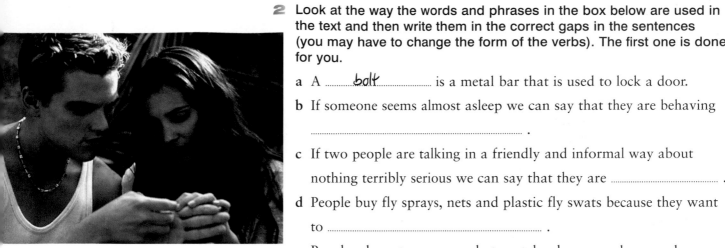

2 Look at the way the words and phrases in the box below are used in the text and then write them in the correct gaps in the sentences (you may have to change the form of the verbs). The first one is done for you.

a A ....*bolt*.................. is a metal bar that is used to lock a door.

b If someone seems almost asleep we can say that they are behaving

....

c If two people are talking in a friendly and informal way about nothing terribly serious we can say that they are ....

d People buy fly sprays, nets and plastic fly swats because they want to ....

e People who get up very early to catch a bus or a plane can be referred to as ....

f People who stay at parties right through the night can be referred to as ....

g Someone who looks excited because they think something good is going to happen is waiting ....

h We call the sound of birds singing in the very early morning the

....

i When a sound is quiet so that you can't hear it very well, we can say that the sound is ....

j When something makes a loud noise when it hits against another surface, we can say that it ....

bolt
chatter
clatter
dawn chorus
die-hard party goers
dozily
early-bird travellers
expectantly
keep the flies at bay
muffled

3 Find the following things in the text and write them in the table.

a three sounds at five o'clock:	
b two sounds at five-thirty:	
c a person the writer looked at:	
d a person who spoke to the writer:	
e Write the rest of the conversation between the American and the writer in complete sentences. (The first line is done for you.)	American: They're banana pancakes. They're the business.

●●● C Text coherence

1 Choose a public holiday in your country. Make notes to show how you would explain it to a foreign visitor. Explain:

a ... when it is. ....

b ... what it's for. ....

c ... what special customs or events happen on that day. ....

d ... what you yourself usually do on that day. ....

2 Look at the pictures below. Do you know what the two festivals are?

Now put the paragraphs that follow in the correct order. (The first one is done for you.)

1 ....*d*....   3 ....   5 ....

2 ....   4 ....   6 ....

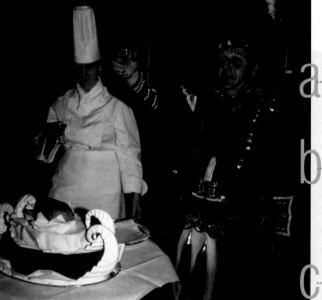

a ⟶ Many national festivals have been celebrated for years, but occasionally new ones come along and old ones gradually disappear. This is unlikely to happen to Burns' Night or St Patrick's Day, however. They are celebrated by too many people for that.

b ⟶ On Burns' Night the guests eat haggis. Haggis is chopped mutton and other ingredients – including liver, heart and oats – encased in sheep's gut, which is boiled before being served. The haggis is brought into the room to the sound of the bagpipes and the chief guest 'addresses' it reciting Burns' poem 'Ode to the Haggis'. After eating, the other guests recite more of Burns' poems, sing Scottish tunes and drink a lot of whisky.

c ⟶ On St Patrick's Day there are big parades, and people wear shamrocks. In some places they add green colouring to the beer and even to rivers and streams. People go out and have 'a good craic' (pronounced 'crack') – Irish for good fun.

d ⟶ Public holidays and festivals are an important part of a country's life. They give everyone a break from routine and they form part of the annual life in that country. Sometimes they celebrate a day in a country's history (Independence Day), commemorate a special person (Columbus Day), mark the passing of time (New Year's Day) or celebrate a religious festival (Christmas, Eid, Diwali).

e ⟶ Another widely celebrated festival is St Patrick's Day (17 March), which celebrates the life of the 5th-century saint. St Patrick was Bishop of Ireland, and it is said that he gave Ireland its national symbol when he illustrated his religious teaching with the shamrock – a three-leafed clover. But the festival is now more than anything a celebration of 'Irishness', whether it takes place in Dublin, Auckland, Melbourne, Montreal or Boston.

f ⟶ Two particular festivals are celebrated far beyond their native land. The first of these, Burns' Night on 25 January, marks the birthday of the Scottish poet Robert Burns (1759–96). It is celebrated by his countrymen and admirers, not only in Scotland but all over the world, from New York to Sydney, from Toronto to Tokyo.

3 Who or what is:

a ... Robert Burns? ....

b ... a haggis? ....

c ... the 'Ode to the Haggis'? ....

d ... St Patrick? ....

e ... a shamrock? ....

f ... 'a good craic'? ....

. . . .

4 Look at the notes you made for Exercise 1. Use them to write an article based on the plan below.

> **Paragraph 1:**
> Introduce the topic.
> ↓
> **Paragraph 2:**
> Give details to illustrate and expand the facts/opinions from the introductory paragraph.
> ↓
> **Paragraphs 3, 4, 5, 6, etc:**
> Give further examples that either add to or contrast with the previous paragraphs.
> ↓
> **Conclusion:**
> **Either** make a general comment, **or** summarise the contents of the previous paragraphs **or** make predictions about the future.

●●● ## A The van

1 Read the text below. You will see that some sentences are missing. Where do the following sentences (a–f) go in the text? (The first one is done for you.)

a Since I started living in my van, I've had feelings I haven't experienced since I was a child. ......**4**......

b I was trying to decide what to do when I saw the advertisement: 'Converted ambulance for sale, £1,600'. ....

c Now I begin to appreciate what the travellers have been telling us all these years. ....

d One problem I've had is what to do about power for my computer. ....

e Parking can be most difficult. ....

f At first I was nervous. ....

No home. No job. No worries.

When he lost his flat, writer CJ Stone decided to 'go on the road'. How will he cope with life in the slow lane?

I didn't wake up one morning and say to myself, 'I think I'll go and live in a van.' It was more accidental than that. First of all I lost my flat and then, at the same time, I discovered I needed a new engine for my car. That meant that I would have to spend £1,000 to get the car back on the road. I suddenly found that I needed, first, somewhere to live and, second, something to travel around in.

1 So I rang the number in the ad and arranged to go and see it. It was love at first sight! I made my decision straight away. Two days later I was the proud owner of a two-litre Ford Transit converted into a camper van.

2 I wasn't sure I could handle it. Where would I park? How would I wash? What would I do in the evenings? I'm the sort of person who needs people around, but you can't give big parties in a van. And how would I cope anyway with life on the road? But I needn't have worried. Well, not much. It's a lot easier than I thought.

3 So far I've slept in several car parks and lay-bys, one or two festival sites and – once or twice – just by the roadside. I haven't yet found the perfect place. I spend a lot of time poring over maps for ideal sites. I ask around among the travellers. And I've no doubt I'll find a site. I'm an optimist – all my life I've always believed I have a place in the world.

4 I suppose it's just the excitement of waking up in the morning, and, for the first few seconds, not knowing where you are. Then you look out of the window, and some new sight greets you: some tree you've never seen before, or some beautiful scenery that makes your heart leap. Living in a flat in the city I missed all that.

5 After all, I'm a writer. To start with I stayed on campsites that had electricity whenever I wanted to work. But it cost money and I couldn't concentrate because everyone else was on holiday and playing games right outside my windows. And then I found the solution: solar panels. That meant I could stay anywhere. Now I'm not only a travelling writer, I'm ecologically sound too.

6 Living in a van is cheap. No rent. No obligations. And on top of that there's the sense of freedom and the happiness that my new lifestyle has given me. Freedom can be addictive. I love being able to go where I want, when I want. It's wonderful to feel that the whole world is your home. No wonder so many people are leaving their houses and going on the road.

2 Answer the following questions.

    a What is CJ Stone's job? ....

    b Where does he live? ....

    c What does he think of it? ....

3 Read the text again and complete the following sentences.

    a CJ Stone decided to live as he does because ....
....

    b CJ Stone worried about his decision because ......
....

    c CJ Stone has parked in many places, such as ......
....

    d CJ Stone loves his new life because ....
....

    e CJ Stone solved his computer problems by ....
....

    f The advantages of living 'on the road' are ....
....

4 Explain the difference between:

    a ... an accident and something that is accidental.

       An accident is something bad that happens when you don't expect it; accidental is when something happens that is not planned.

    b ... a park and a car park. ....
....
....
....

    c ... a site and a sight. ....
....

    d ... a road sign and the roadside. ....
....
....

    e ... an optimist and a pessimist. ....
....
....

    f ... a campsite and a camper van. ....
....
....

Language in chunks

5 Look at these phrases from the text. Use them in the gaps.

> a sense of freedom   cope with   have no doubt [that]
> make a decision   spend a lot of time [doing something]

    a I can't .... computers. I just don't understand them.

    b He .... writing stories on his computer. He never seems to stop!

    c I'm not sure whether to buy a camper van, but I'm going to .... soon.

    d Walking in the countryside gives me ....

    e He wants to marry her. He .... she's the one for him.

●●● B Poems

1 Read the following poem, 'The Confession'. What is the correct
order of the three verses. Write the numbers 1–3 in the brackets.

The Confession
by Brian Patten

When he showed her the photograph again, she said,

[ ] 'It was a July afternoon.
The day was hot and my body hummed.
I was bored and in search of an adventure
That seemed beyond you.

[ ] 'Yes, I remember taking it.
I was incredibly young then.
You handed me the camera
And telling me over and over how to use it
You posed, smiling stiffly.
You were so pompous, so blind to everything.

[ ] 'Yet how can I forget that day?
Look closer at the photograph.
See there in the background,
In the corner behind you
The other boy, grinning so openly.'

Check the answer key. Did you get the order right?

2 Make sure you know the meaning of the words in the box below and then use them to complete the poem.

clothes
clumsily
inside
nothing
patiently
poor
smirks
wearing

I Am Completely Different
by Karoda Saburo

I am completely different.
Though I am (a) .... the same tie as yesterday,
am as (b) .... as yesterday,
as good for (c) .... as yesterday,
today
I am completely different.
Though I am wearing the same (d) ....,
am as drunk as yesterday,
living as (e) .... as yesterday, nevertheless
today
I am completely different.

Ah –
I (f) .... close my eyes
on all the grins and (g) ....
on all the twisted smiles and horse laughs –
and glimpse then, (h) .... me,
one beautiful white butterfly
fluttering towards tomorrow.

Check the correct answers in the key.

. . . .

3 Tick the correct column for each of the questions below.

Which poem:	'The Confession'	'I Am Completely Different'
a ... talks about clothes?		
b ... talks about an incident in the past?		
c ... has three people in it?		
d ... is written by a poet talking about himself or herself?		
e ... is more optimistic than pessimistic?		
f ... is about a long-kept secret?		
g ... talks about two people smiling very differently?		
h ... do you like best?		

●●● C Letter writing

1 Study the letter below and make notes about the following questions.

a Where is Brenda writing from? ....

b How did she and Mariel get there? ....

c How did she feel when she first arrived? How does she feel now?................................

....

d What differences are there between Brenda's and Mariel's characters?.........................

....

e What is Brenda's job? What is Mariel's?...

f Who is David? ....

g How formal is the letter? How do you know? ....

Flat 3
156 Centenary Road
Mumbai
India

15th June

Dear Rosemary,

I've just received your letter – thanks. It was nice to hear from you.

Well, we've been here for three weeks already. I still can't believe it. But things have definitely improved since the bus left us at the roadside on that first day. For a minute I wanted to turn round and go home again. You know me, I'm a great pessimist. But Mariel always thinks everything is going to be fine. In less than a day she had found us a flat and here we are.

I've found myself a job giving private conversation classes. Not quite what I'm used to, but it's still teaching and my students are lovely. Mariel hasn't got a job yet, but she's made contact with various people in the film industry here and hopes she'll get work soon.

So the big news is, we've made our decision. We've decided to stay. This is our home.

Please give my love to David and the kids. Why not come and visit us soon?

Lots of love,
Brenda

2 Would you use the following in letters which are *Formal* (F) or *Informal* (I) or *Neutral* (neither formal nor informal) (N)? Circle the correct choice for each.

a	Hi Rosemary	F I N	
b	Dear Mrs Forrest	F I N	
c	Dear James	F I N	
d	Dear Ms Forrest	F I N	
e	Dear Sir or Madam	F I N	
f	With best wishes	F I N	
g	Lots of love	F I N	
h	Yours sincerely	F I N	
i	Yours faithfully	F I N	
j	Love	F I N	
k	Thanks for your letter.	F I N	
l	Thank you very much for your letter.	F I N	
m	Please give my love to David and the kids.	F I N	
n	I look forward to hearing from you.	F I N	🔑

3 You are going to write a letter. Make notes on the following.

a Choose somewhere in the world you like the sound of. Imagine that you are now living there. ....

....

b How did you get there? ....

c What kind of job do you normally do? Have you found something similar in your new place? ....

....

d Where are you living in your new country? What kind of a place is it? ....

e What English-speaking friend or relative (real or imaginary) could you write to? ....

....

Now, using your notes, write a letter to your English-speaking friend or relative. Use the language from Brenda's letter to help you.

....

....

....

....

....

....

....

●●● A Three women

1 Read about these famous women. Copy and complete the table on page 37 for each one.

FAMOUS FEMALES

Mary Read, one of the most famous female pirates in history, was born in London in 1690. Her father died when she was young and Mary's mother raised her as a boy. Only male children could inherit money so Mary was disguised as a boy so that she would inherit her grandmother's money.

When Mary was 13 she joined a ship, still dressed as a man. A few years later she joined the British army (as a man) and was sent to fight the French in Holland. There she fell in love with one of her fellow soldiers — and had to reveal her secret, much to everyone's surprise!

When her husband died, Mary put on men's clothes again and joined a ship going to the West Indies. But the ship was captured by English pirates, led by Jack Rackham and Anne Bonney. Mary decided to become a member of the pirate crew. She fell in love again, this time with a soldier they had captured, and was married. But their honeymoon was short because Mary and her fellow pirates, Jack and Anne, were taken prisoner near Jamaica and were sentenced to death. Mary was saved from death because she was pregnant, but she died in prison in 1720.

Cristina Sánchez was one of the only female bullfighters, or 'matadors', of modern times. She was forced to stop fighting bulls because of criticism — many people thought that bullfighting was only for men.

Women in Spain have fought bulls since the 18th century, but a law in 1908 banned them on the grounds of 'decency and public morality'. The ban was lifted briefly in the 1930s when Spain became a republic, but was put back again by the dictator Francisco Franco. The ban was lifted again after Franco's death in 1976 — but even then most women only fought on horseback. Cristina fought on foot.

Cristina was born in Madrid, Spain, in 1972. She started her bullfighting career in South America when she was only 20. She attracted a lot of attention and soon became a matador back in Spain. However, Cristina was frequently criticised by male bullfighters. A lot of people believed that women in the ring were unlucky. 'Women should be in the kitchen, backing up men. It's unnatural for them to fight,' said Jesulin de Ubrique, a typical critic. Many male bullfighters refused to appear with her.

Cristina Sánchez retired in 1999 because she was fed up with the attitude of the other matadors and some of the public. But, almost certainly, she won't be the last female matador.

Calamity Jane was a heroine of the American Wild West, famous for her bravery. A film was made about her in 1953, starring Doris Day.

Calamity Jane's real name was Martha Jane Cannary and she was born in 1852 in Missouri, USA. Her parents were farmers. As a young girl she could ride a horse and shoot a gun as well as any man. In the 1870s, dressed as a man, she fought with the army against the Native Americans. During a fierce battle, the captain was shot and fell from his horse. She lifted him on to her own horse and saved him. When he recovered, the captain said, 'I name you Calamity Jane, the heroine of the plains.'

In 1876 Calamity Jane met Wild Bill Hickock and they settled in the town of Deadwood, Dakota. The same year, Wild Bill was shot in the back of the head while playing cards in a saloon bar.

Calamity Jane left Deadwood. For a time she raised cattle and kept an inn. Then she moved to California, and later to El Paso, Texas, where she married Clinton Burke. They had a daughter, but the marriage was not a success. Calamity Jane never had much money and died a poor woman in 1903. She was buried in Deadwood next to Wild Bill Hickock, as she had requested.

Name
a Dates (birth/death):
b Nationality:
c What was special about her:
d Main events in her life:
e Important people in her life:
f How/why her career ended:

2 Who was:

a ... captured by English pirates? ....

....

b ... criticised by male bullfighters? ....

....

c ... known for her bravery? ....

d ... disguised as a boy? ....

e ... buried next to Wild Bill Hickock? ....

f ... shot in a saloon bar? ....

Language in chunks

3 Complete the sentences using phrases from the box. (You might have to change the tense of some verbs.)

> much to my surprise   on foot   on horseback   the ban was lifted
>
> fall in love with   settle in

a My great-grandfather was a village carpenter. His family was very poor. As a boy he had to go to school ....

b He .... my great-grandmother when he saw her at a dance.

c My great-grandfather wanted to live in the capital city, but in those days you were not allowed to move away from your own village. However, ... just after my great-grandparents got married.

d In the end they .... the capital city. They rode there ....

e I wrote an essay about my great-grandfather for a competition at school. .... I won first prize for it.

●●● B A dangerous husband

1 Read the information about Henry VIII. Put his wives in chronological order, that is to say, the order in which they were his wives. The following rhyme, which British school children learn, may help you.

Divorced, beheaded, died

Divorced, beheaded, survived.

1 ....

2 ....

3 ....

4 ....

5 ....

6 ....

Do not marry this man!

Being married to England's King Henry VIII was a dangerous business. It could easily cost you your life!

Henry VIII (1491–1547) is one of the most famous characters in English history. As a young man he was handsome and extremely athletic, and according to contemporary accounts, everyone thought he was extremely attractive. He was a brilliant horseman, and a superb shot with a bow and arrow. He was expert at an early version of the game of tennis, and was also an accomplished musician. The famous tune 'Greensleeves' is said to have been written by him, though there is no proof of this.

The one thing Henry was not very good at was having sons. He married six different women to try and produce a male heir to the throne, but his only son from all these marriages died when he was just 14 years old. However, his two daughters both became queens of England, so if he had only lived long enough, he might not have been so worried. In alphabetical order, Henry's six wives were as follows.

Anne Boleyn (1507–36)

Henry fell in love with her when he was still married to his first wife, Catherine of Aragon. Catherine had failed to give him a son, so he divorced her to marry Anne. Anne had a daughter called Elizabeth (who later became Queen Elizabeth I) but no son. When Henry got tired of her they found a reason to accuse her of crimes against the king. She was found guilty and executed by having her head cut off.

Anne of Cleves (1515–57)

After Jane Seymour's death Henry was extremely unhappy. But an artist brought him back a portrait of Anne of Cleves. She seemed very good-looking, and marriage to her was good politics. But when Henry saw her he thought she was ugly and never liked her. They were married for less than a year before Henry divorced her.

Catherine of Aragon (1485–1536)

Daughter of Ferdinand V of Castile (Spain). She married Arthur, eldest son of Henry VII of England, but when he died she married his brother Henry VIII. She had one daughter (Mary) who later became queen of England before her half-sister Elizabeth. However Catherine had no sons so Henry divorced her to marry Anne Boleyn, a woman he'd fallen in love with.

Catherine Howard (1521–42)

Catherine Howard was the niece of the Duke of Norfolk, one of the most important men in the country after the king. She was married to Henry in 1540, just after his disastrous marriage to Anne of Cleves. But less than two years later Catherine was accused of loving someone else and was executed.

Catherine Parr (1512–48)

Henry's last wife was the one, people said, who could best control the old king. She was sweet and kind, and Henry, who was by now ill and fat, loved her in his own way. Catherine was still alive when Henry died. She remarried but died in childbirth a year later.

Jane Seymour (1509–37)

Henry fell in love with Jane Seymour while he was still married to Anne Boleyn. As soon as Anne had been executed he married Jane and in 1537, a year later, she produced a son, Edward VI, but died herself 12 days later. On the death of Henry, Edward became king at the age of nine, but died five years later.

2 Look at the way the following words and phrases are used in the text and then write them in the gaps in the sentences.

accomplished
athletic
contemporary accounts
control
died in childbirth
disastrous
good politics
horseman
niece
male heir
proof
superb shot

a A boy who will become king after the present king dies is his

....

b A piece of information that shows beyond doubt that something is true is called ....

c Historians talk about things written at the same time as they happened as ....

d If you want someone to do exactly what you tell them and only what you tell them you will try to .... them.

e My brother's daughter is my ....

f When someone can hit a target every time (with a gun or a bow and arrow) we call them a ....

g When a woman dies at the same time as her baby is born we say she ....

h When somebody is very good and experienced at something they are called ....

i When someone is very good at physical sports we often call them ....

j When someone makes a decision that will help them or their country we can say that it is ....

k When something is a complete failure we call it ....

l A man who regularly rides a horse is called a ....

3 Complete the following table with the information required.

a Any three things Henry was good at:	1 ....
	2 ....
	3 ....
b The names of Henry's children in order of birth:	1 ....
	2 ....
	3 ....
c Write the names of Henry's children in the order that they were king or queen:	1 ....
	2 ....
	3 ....
d The name of the wife who lived the longest:	....
e The name of the wife who had a son:	....
f The name of the wife who Henry thought was ugly:	....
g The name of the wife married to Henry's brother:	....

●●● C Biography

1 Imagine you are going to interview someone. Write questions in English to find out the following biographical information.

a Name: ....

b Date and place of birth: ....

c Background (nationality, where they have lived, education):

....

....

....

....

d Important events in their life: ....

....

....

....

....

e Most recent important event: ....

....

....

....

....

f How they would describe themselves: ....

....

....

....

....

g Interests: ....

....

....

....

....

h Future important events or hopes: ....

....

....

....

....

2 Complete one of the following tasks.

   a Use your questions to interview someone who speaks English.
     Make a note of their answers.
   b Make notes about yourself or about someone you know in answer
     to the questions.

You can write your notes in the following table.

a Name:	
b Date and place of birth:	
c Background (nationality, where they have lived, education):	
d Important events in their life:	
e Most recent important event:	
f How they would describe themselves:	
g Interests:	
h Future important events or hopes:	

3 Use your notes to write three short paragraphs. You can follow this plan.

Introduce the person, their background, and early events.

↓

Describe the person and their interests.

↓

Talk about the most recent events in their life and discuss what the future holds for them.

UNIT 7

●●● **A** Resolutions

Look at the exercises on page 43 and then read this text.

Home • **Articles** • **Forums** • **Chat** • **Classifieds** • **Newsletters** • **Help**

Subjects

ESSENTIALS

Science of health

Healthfinder

Health Directory

Health Books

Glossary of Terms

Eating Disorders

Personality Disorders

Anxiety

Panic

Grief

Ageing

Health psychology

Depression

Stress Management

Self-Help

How to make those New Year's resolutions stick
by Dr Pauline Wallin

Every year on 1 and 2 January, millions of us make New Year's resolutions. We'll say we are going to quit smoking or that we'll join a gym. We'll go on a diet or promise ourselves that from now on we're going to spend more time on housework or that we're going to cut down on all the chocolate we eat. But by 2 February, most of these resolutions will be no more than a distant memory and we'll be behaving just the same as we were when the last year ended.

One reason why people abandon all their promises and resolutions is that it's easy to say we're going to do something (or not going to do something) but much harder to go on and on doing it (or not doing it) – especially if it is difficult or uncomfortable for us. OK, everyone may need a bit of a rest from all the eating and drinking over Christmas and the New Year, but a few weeks later our appetites have returned and we start to feel deprived. That's when we are most at risk – especially if the results of our dieting or not smoking are not immediately visible.

But don't despair! If you're thinking of making New Year's resolutions, first be sure you're ready for the challenge, and then read on for tips on how to increase your chances of success.

1   Examine your motivation for change. At the end of a long night, after a large meal, you say, 'That's it, I'm going on a diet tomorrow,' but the chances are you won't feel the same in 24 hours. However, if you are realistic and accept that change will be difficult, you will stay motivated for longer.
2   Set realistic goals. Habits and behaviours that are changed gradually have a greater chance of success than those that are changed so drastically that your mind and body just can't cope.
3   Focus on the programme rather than the goal. If you decide to control your eating, your goal for the day is not to lose a specific number of pounds, but to stick to your programme. Such focus on your behaviour will help you feel in control of your life. You will gain satisfaction from making sensible choices several times throughout the day.
4   Be positive about your physical symptoms. When you give up smoking you'll feel strange. See that as a good sign of your body getting rid of the drug, not as something unpleasant.
5   Stick to your decisions. Yesterday you said, 'I'm going to the gym at eight o'clock tomorrow morning.' But now it's quarter past seven in the morning and you don't feel like getting up. Tough! You'll never stick to those resolutions if you don't keep trying when it's difficult.
6   Nobody's perfect! You'll probably mess up from time to time. But you mustn't give in just because of that. Say to yourself, 'I'm going on with this – today, tomorrow and the next day. I'm not a quitter.'
7   If you're waiting for a more convenient time to begin to change your behaviour, that change won't happen. It's almost never convenient to change ingrained habits, so if you're going to do it, start right now. And then things will get better sooner!

1 Read the information on the right about what happens at New Year in the UK. Is it the same as New Year in your country?

NEW YEAR'S EVE is 31st December. Many people go to parties or stay up and watch the New Year celebrations on television. It is common for people to make New Year's resolutions – promises to behave better in the following year (e.g. to stop eating so much chocolate, to take up exercise etc). New Year's Day is 1st January. It is always a public holiday. Most people stay at home, recovering from the evening before.

2 Why do you think people find it difficult to stick to New Year's resolutions (to keep the promises they made)? Make notes about what advice you would give someone about how to (a) stop doing something bad or (b) start doing something better.

....
....
....
....
....
....

3 Read the website text by Dr Pauline Wallin, opposite. Does she agree with you?

4 Read the text again and find:

a ... five resolutions that people sometimes make.

1 ....

2 ....

3 ....

4 ....

5 ....

b ... three reasons why sticking to resolutions is difficult.

1 ....

2 ....

3 ....

Language in chunks

5 Complete the following sentences with these phrases from the text.

| on a diet   a distant memory   at risk   can't cope   in control of |
| gain satisifaction   feel like   nobody's perfect |

a 'What's the matter? You look worried.' 'I've got too much work just now. I just ....'

b 'Do you remember your tenth birthday clearly?' 'No, it's just ....'

c 'What's the matter?' 'I don't feel .... my life. Everything is going wrong.'

d 'I didn't do very well in my maths exam!' 'Oh, never mind, ...'

e 'Are you saying I'm overweight?' 'No! You don't need to go ....'

f 'Are you staying in tonight?' 'Yes, I don't .... going to Shelly's party.'

g 'You really think I can climb that mountain?' 'Yes I do, and you'll also .... when you reach the top.'

h 'We've hardly sold any tickets for our show.' 'I know. It's .... of being cancelled.'

●●● B The best place to get married?

1 Read the newspaper article, and then write the correct names under the pictures below.

a .... b ....

c .... d ....

Marathon marriage just the tip of the iceberg

When Angela Stratford agreed to marry Nigel Jones, they decided to do it in style. They're just one of the many couples who choose an out-of-the-ordinary experience for the most important day in their lives.

Nigel Jones, 48, and his 34-year-old wife Angela had been together for six years before they became husband and wife in 2001. They ran hand in hand for 25 miles of the 2001 London marathon before stopping at a statue called Cleopatra's Needle, where family and friends cheered as they were married. After the ceremony they ran the last mile of the race waving a banner that said 'Just Married'. Later they had a wedding reception at a hotel in Greenwich.

Angela met Nigel at a running club – and thought of the marathon wedding. 'I just thought it was the perfect way to get married,' she said. But she only agreed to become Nigel's wife when he could run as fast as she could. 'I said only a man who can catch me will be able to marry me,' she said. 'He ran and ran, and eventually got to my level, and we started doing races together. I wasn't interested in anyone who didn't want to race!'

The bride wore a knee-length cream wedding dress with veil and cream gloves. Her husband-to-be wore shorts, a jacket and a pretend shirt and tie.

Bishop Jonathan Blake who conducted the wedding ceremony said, 'I have married people underwater, over the Internet, on boats and aeroplanes. I think it is wonderful that people can be free to express themselves, choose a service and an interesting setting that has more meaning for them. But I can't imagine getting married after running 25 miles.'

But if you don't fancy running a marathon to get married, you could always decide to go abroad for that special day and travel companies are now doing their best to persuade young couples to do just that. 'With the average cost of a wedding in the UK being about £12,000,' according to Sasha Pliotnov, a designer who specialises in marriage ceremonies, 'quite a few people are beginning to realise that it's a lot cheaper to fly off with just a few special friends and family to some exotic location and get married on a beautiful island or in some other romantic setting.'

There is no limit to the number and type of locations on offer. Award-winning tour operator *Kuoni*, for example, advertises 24 different packages. Its most popular one is the Triton Hotel in Sri Lanka. *Thomson Cruises* suggests a wedding on board ship – and you don't even have to travel far for the honeymoon. *Sandals Luxury Resorts* offer all sorts of wedding packages in the Caribbean, and *My Travel Group* offers anything from an Austrian chapel to the Australian outback.

Of course if you don't want to go abroad, you could always get married in a hot air balloon, on an ice-skating rink, up a mountain, or in a tree. They've all been done.

None of this impresses Ronald and Daisy Crabtree who got married on the same day as Nigel and Angela's interrupted marathon wedding. 'We got married in church,' Roger said, 'because that's the tradition. Daisy wore a traditional wedding dress and I wore a morning coat and a top hat. That's how people have always got married and it seemed the right thing for us too. We had a lovely day, something we will always remember.'

2 According to the text, who:

a ... completed a race after they were married?

....

b ... encourages people to get married on a boat?

....

c ... got married after the man answered a challenge successfully?

....

d ... has been an official at many strange weddings?

....

e ... knows the price of weddings?

....

f ... met in 1995?

....

g ... offers weddings in Austria?

....

h ... wants people to get married in Sri Lanka?

....

i ... will always remember their wedding?

....

j ... wore a traditional wedding dress?

....

3 Look at the way the phrases in the box are used in the text and then use them to fill the gaps in these sentences.

exotic location
got to my level
hand in hand
in style
out of the ordinary
romantic setting
the tip of an iceberg
wedding package
wedding reception

a A location that makes people think of love or feel loving is sometimes described as a ....

b A phrase to describe a small part of a much bigger situation is

....

c An all-inclusive programme you pay for when you book your wedding through a travel agent can be called a

....

d An unusual, interesting and often foreign place can be referred to as an ....

e When he reached the same standard as me he

....

f If something is very unusual or different we say it is

....

g If you do something in a way that people admire and/or which costs a lot of money you could say that you are doing it

....

h The party after two people are married is called a

....

i When two people hold each other's hand we say they are

....

●●● C Invitations

1 Look at the following invitations (1–4) and then answer the questions.

❶

Mr and Mrs Gurney
have great pleasure in inviting you to the wedding of their daughter
Katherine
to
Gerald McWhitney

At St George's Parish Church
Clifford Chambers
On April 1
At 11 am
and afterwards at 13 Rambsborough Drive, Stratford-upon-Avon,
Warwickshire CV37 2JE

RSVP

❷

Party! Party!
Come and celebrate Rosie's birthday
21 February, 8 'til late
Bring a bottle
The Q Club, at the end of Station Road
The coolest party in town.

BE THERE!

❸

Carol, Gita, Sasha & Miguel

Would like to invite you

For: drinks

On: Saturday August 7

From: 7.30 pm onwards

At: 121 Lion Drive, Peckham

Tel: 020 7654 3729
email: gita.sahkil@richmond.com

Please let us know if you can come.

❹

From: Jed <mortonj@shaftesbury.com>
To: Maureen <malatski@nfm.com>
Cc:
Bcc:
Subject: great party
Any chance you can come to my party next Saturday, starting at about 7.30? Everyone's going to be there. It would be great if you could come too :-)
Bring a bottle and something to eat. And don't worry, Shiona can come too if she wants.
C U next Saturday?
Jed
BTW do you have Matt's email address? I want to ask him too (if that's OK?).

a Which is the most formal? ....

b Which is the most casual? ....

c Are the people who are sending the invitations young or old?

1 .... 2 .... 3 .... 4 ....

2 Read the invitations again and answer the following questions.

a What information has to go on any invitation?

....

....

b What wording is used to invite the person in each case?

....

....

....

....

c What does the invitee have to do in each case? Is it always the same thing?

....

....

....

....

d What do the following mean in an email?

1 :-) ....

2 C U ....

3 BTW ....

3 Imagine that you are planning a party to celebrate an event such as the end of a course, New Year's Eve, or an important birthday. You have unlimited money for your party.

a Decide:

• where the party should be. ....

• when it should start and end. ....

• what music there should be. ....

• what food and drink you want. ....

• what will make your party special – one that people will

   remember. ....

   ....

b Write an invitation for the party you have decided to hold. Base it on one of the examples (1–4) in Exercise 1.

●●● A Graffiti

1 Read the text and then think about these questions.

a What is graffiti? ....

b What is most people's attitude to it? .... 🔑

GRAFFITI - STREET ART OR STREET SHAME?

Tags

It all started in 1972 in New York. A painted symbol – TAKI 183 – began to appear on walls and on the side of trains. It soon became clear that TAKI 183 was the signature – or 'tag' as it is called – of a single individual who was painting anything he could. Since then, graffiti has spread all over the world, with paintings getting more and more ambitious. It is done at night on walls, bridges, public buildings and the sides of trains. Most artists have their own tag, which they keep for as long as they work – or until the police catch them. Then they have to invent a new tag for themselves.

Penalties

When the police catch graffiti artists for the first time they usually give them a small fine or a caution, but for second, third or fourth offences the penalties can get more serious.

The Newcastle Two

A few years ago, two teenagers were prosecuted in Newcastle upon Tyne in the north of England. They were sent to a young offenders' institution for three months. According to the police, they had caused £30,000 worth of damage to public property.

Simon Sunderland

Simon Sunderland was sent to prison last week for five years, one of the most serious punishments ever given to a graffiti artist. At his trial in Sheffield the judge said, 'If the people of this area could see the photographic evidence of the damage you have caused they would probably be very shocked. The message from this court is clear. If you set out to target and spray the buildings of the people of South Yorkshire, you will go to prison for a long time.'

Sunderland's career started after he asked Barnsley Council to provide walls for graffiti artists. The council refused and so he started spraying any buildings he could find using the tags 'fisto' or 'fista'. He worked at night in his favourite colours of red, black and silver. His paintings appeared on hundreds, possibly thousands, of sites. It cost the local council £500,000 a year to clean up the buildings he had painted on.

On one occasion, Sunderland sprayed a bus that had broken down. On another, a man saw him at work and went up to him to complain. Sunderland turned round and sprayed the man! In a magazine article recently he said, 'I look for walls wherever I go. It gives me a buzz. It feels like people know you!'

Things came to an end when a policeman saw him spraying a motorway bridge. When the police went to his house they discovered hundreds of spray-paint cans and maps of the areas he worked in.

What's your view?

Is graffiti ugly or is it art? Should we celebrate it or condemn it? Who should pay to have it cleaned? Should graffiti artists be sent to prison? Write to us and tell us what you think.

2 Answer the following questions.

a What is a tag? ....

b Who are the Newcastle Two? ....

....

c Who was sent to prison for five years? ....

d Who refused to give graffiti artists walls to paint

on? ....

e Which tags did Simon Sunderland use?

....

f Who spent £500,000 a year, and why?

....

g Who complained to Simon Sunderland and

what happened? ....

....

h Who saw Simon Sunderland painting a

motorway bridge? ....

3 Find words or phrases in the text with the following meanings.
The first letter of each answer is provided for you.

a the way people write their name, usually on a
cheque or at the end of a letter: s.............................

b to make or design something new for the first
time: i.............................

c punishments for breaking a law or rule:
p.............................

d actions that are against the law:
o............................. .

e accused officially: p.............................

f places: s.............................

g to produce a stream of paint from a can:
s.............................

4 Write a paragraph in answer to one of the following questions.

a Graffiti – is it street art or street shame?

b Was the judge right to send Simon
Sunderland to prison?

Language in chunks

5 Use expressions from the box below to complete the story of Bill Adams, which follows.

| according to the police | go to prison for a long time | it gives me a buzz | it soon became clear |
| on one occasion | things came to an end | went up to him |

Next week, 18-year-old Bill Adams goes on trial for robbery. (a) .... , he is one of the busiest criminals in the country.

Bill likes to rob buildings when people are in them. '(b) .... to take things when people are in the next room,' he told police investigators. (c) .... he went into a house where a party was going on. A party guest (d) .... and talked to him for five minutes, but Bill managed to get away from him.

However, (e) .... when someone saw him climbing through a window. The police arrived and arrested him. When they went to his parents' house they found hundreds of stolen items. (f) .... that Bill was no ordinary thief.

The police hope that Adams will (g) .... , but Bill remains optimistic. 'I'm young,' he said, 'I'm sure they'll give me a second chance.'

••• B From graffiti to art fame

An extraordinary life

How a New York graffiti artist became the darling of the art world, but did not live to tell the tale

David Bowie and Jeffrey Wright as Andy Warhol and Jean-Michel Basquiat

Jean-Michel Basquiat
Untitiled (Skull), 1981
acrylic and mixed media on canvas
81 x 69 ¼ inches
The Eli and Edythe L. Broad collection
Photograph © Douglas M. Parker Studio
The Broad Art Foundation

Jean-Michel Basquiat, who was born in New York in 1960, was the son of a Haitian father and a Puerto Rican mother. As a child he liked drawing pictures, and because they were good his mother encouraged his interest.

At the age of 18 Basquiat left home and quit school just before he was due to graduate. He had nowhere special to live. Sometimes he would sleep in a cardboard box in Thompkins Square Park. Sometimes he would stay with friends. He played in a band, and started doing graffiti, tagging walls and subway cars with the signature 'SAMO'. But he also painted – a curious mixture of words and images, of western art and the traditions of Haiti, Puerto Rico and Africa. It seemed to many that he was searching for some kind of identity.

Basquiat's paintings were first shown in a joint exhibition in 1980, and immediately people started to get interested – very interested. Soon he was surrounded by agents, gallery owners, journalists and many other people who were desperate to make him famous and make money out of him. His fame spread like wildfire and everyone was talking about him. There were exhibitions of his work all over America. He dated the (not yet famous) pop star Madonna and became a great friend of Andy Warhol, one of the giants of the New York art scene. In 1986 he went to the Ivory Coast in Africa. In 1988 he had simultaneous exhibitions in Paris and New York. But that was the year when it all came to an end. Jean-Michel died of a drug overdose at the age of 27.

Basquiat is still remembered today, not just because he was the first black artist to have real success in the white world of art, but also because he was a fascinating, beautiful man. One writer wrote of him as a 'radiant child'. John Seed, who worked as his assistant when he was at the height of his powers, says that he was 'completely original'. He remembers the first day he met him. Even though he was successful Jean-Michel lived in a room with only two pieces of furniture: a bed and a television. There were books and paintings all over the floor. He remembers too how Basquiat turned up late at his first big exhibition, listening to his personal stereo. He was not comfortable with large crowds, yet many people loved him as one of the most creative and kind people they had ever met.

One fellow artist who knew and worked with Jean-Michel was Julian Schnabel. Nearly ten years after his friend's death he made a film called, simply, Basquiat, a celebration of an extraordinary life. It stars Jeffrey Wright as Jean-Michel, David Bowie as Andy Warhol and Courtney Love as a Madonna-like character. There are other roles for well-known actors such as Dennis Hopper

One scene shows Basquiat behaving as Schnabel wants to remember him. Jean-Michel is in a restaurant with a girlfriend. Suddenly he pours syrup all over the table, spreads it with a paper napkin, and then, with his fork, draws a perfect portrait of the girl sitting opposite him. Then he smiles and he is happy.

1 Read the text opposite and then complete this table.
The first answer is done for you.

Name:	Jean–Michel Basquiat
Dates (of birth/death):	
Place of birth:	
Parents' nationalities:	
Occupations mentioned (3):	
Places where exhibitions were held:	
Name of the film about the main character:	
Actors in the film:	

2 Read through the text again. Now note down the names that go with each of these descriptions.

a He was born in New York. ....

b It was the place where Basquiat slept in a cardboard box.

....

c He used the tag 'SAMO'. ....

d She had an affair with Basquiat. ....

e He was a famous friend of Basquiat. ....

f He lived for 27 years. ....

g He was Basquiat's assistant. ....

h He was an artist who worked with Basquiat. ....

i He made a film about Basquiat. ....

3 Look at the way the following words and phrases are used in the text and then write them in the correct gaps (a–h). You may have to change some of the words.

a .... is a thick, sweet liquid.

b .... is another word for a picture, photograph etc.

c If someone doesn't really know who they are but wants to know, they may well be ....

d If someone leaves education before the time they are due to finish, we can say that they ....

e If someone supports you in something you like doing and helps you to do more of it, we can say they ....

f Two things that happen at the same time are .... happenings.

g When someone is the principal actor in a film we say the film .... them.

h When someone is doing their best work (and probably being very successful) we can say that they are ....

at the height of (his) powers

encouraged (his) interest

image

quit school

searching for some kind of identity

simultaneous

star (verb)

syrup

●●● C Making text work

1 Read the text. What is the connection between:

a ... the dog and the rabbit? ....

b ... Mr Jesperson and the rabbit? ....

c ... Mr Jesperson and the dog? ....

d ... Mrs Ramsey and the fence? ....

e ... Mr Jesperson and Harmony? ....

f ... Mrs Ramsey and Mr Jesperson? ....

Neighbour bites dog in fence dispute

1 A 47-year-old man, William Jesperson, bit <u>his</u> neighbour's dog in a dispute about <u>her</u> garden fence yesterday. Mrs Carol Ramsey has complained to the police and <u>her</u> dog needed four stitches.

2 The argument between William Jesperson and Carol Ramsey started when Mrs Ramsey took down the fence between <u>their</u> two gardens. She told <u>her</u> neighbour she was going to replace it with a newer one but she has not yet done so because, she claims, she cannot afford to.

3 When the fence was removed Mrs Ramsey's dog used Mr Jesperson's garden to play in, on one occasion frightening <u>his</u> two-year-old son, according to <u>his</u> wife Harmony. Despite repeated complaints, Mrs Ramsey did nothing, and when the dog chased Mr Jesperson's pet rabbit, the outraged father and pet-lover took action.

4 Local police are investigating the incident.

2 Read the newspaper article again and then answer the following questions.

    a What tense is used in the headline? ....

    ....

    b Which kinds of word are missing from the headline? ....

    ....

    c What is the purpose of each paragraph?

        1 ....

        2 ....

        3 ....

        4 ....

    d Look at the underlined words. What are they? ....

    ....

    e Who or what do each of the underlined words refer to?

    ....

    ....

    ....

    ....

3 Choose one of the topics below.

       • graffiti
       • street performers
       • a dispute between neighbours

    a Invent a story for a newspaper article about one of these topics.

    b Make notes for the article, showing what each paragraph should contain. How are you going to finish the article?

    ....

    ....

    ....

    ....

    c Write a headline for your article.

    d Write the article.

    ....

    ....

    ....

    ....

    ....

    ....

●●● A Talking bodies

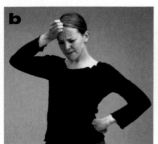

Talking bodies

We know what our words mean, but how good are we at understanding body language?
Sarah Frost reports

When you talk to people face to face, you communicate with much more than your words and the sound of your voice. You also give an enormous amount of information through the language of your body. In fact, in any communication, over 50 per cent of the information you give comes from your body language. We all use body language, whether consciously or subconsciously, and it can tell people more about us than we might want them to know.

The use of body language can be a powerful indicator of how you feel. This is often a conscious way of communicating. Smiling shows you are happy; shrugging your shoulders tells someone that you don't know something or that you don't care, and waving is a way of saying 'hello' or 'goodbye'. There are other gestures, however, that give information without you realising. Crossing your arms may indicate that you are relaxed, bored or want to protect yourself; scratching your head might show you are puzzled; tapping your foot might mean you are feeling impatient, and fidgeting might show you are nervous.

When people are good friends or when two people agree with each other, they often echo each other's body language, crossing their legs in the same way or using the same gestures. This is often done subconsciously but a person might copy someone else's body movements consciously to make fun of them!

How often you look into someone's eyes also sends powerful messages. We make eye contact more often in a conversation with friends than with strangers and lack of eye contact can indicate nervousness. In general conversation, we look at each other for short periods of time, but when the topic becomes more personal we often look away. Deep eye contact is usually only used for very strong emotions such as love or anger. If someone avoids eye contact altogether when speaking, it might mean they are not telling the truth.

The physical distance between speakers can indicate a number of things. Standing close together, for example, can suggest intimacy, whilst distance may indicate formality or a lack of interest. Standing close to someone may be quite appropriate in some situations, such as an informal party, but completely out of place in others, such as a meeting with your boss.

Body language can sometimes get you into trouble when you travel abroad. Smiling is an almost universal signal of pleasure or welcome, but other gestures may have different meanings in different cultures. The same gesture, used in different cultures, can mean 'OK', 'zero', 'fantastic result', 'money' – or something much more insulting! In Britain, people often raise their eyebrows to suggest surprise or interest; when they bite their lip we think they may be uncertain or worried; when they clench their teeth or their fist we know they are angry.

So when you next talk to somebody – be careful. Your body may be saying a lot more than you think!

1 Look at the pictures on the opposite page. Think about what the people are feeling, and how you know what they are feeling.

2 Read the text opposite and then notice the body language mentioned in paragraph 2 of the article. Now write down the body language in each picture (a–f). The first one has been done for you.

a .*crossing your arms.* b .... c ....

d .... e .... f .... 🔑

3 Match these words from the text with the following meanings.

universal
subconsciously
protect yourself
strangers
intimacy
uncertain
fidgeting

a a close personal relationship: ....

b all over the world: ....

c confused: ....

d making a lot of small, restless movements, usually with your hands:

....

e people we don't know: ....

f to do something without being aware: ....

g to make yourself safe from danger: .... 🔑

4 According to the text, why might people:

a ... smile? ....

b ... raise their eyebrows? ....

c ... bite their lips? ....

d ... shrug their shoulders? ....

e ... cross their arms? ....

f ... wave? ....

g ... scratch their head? .... 🔑

Language in chunks

5 Match the phrases in the first column with their opposites in the second column. Draw lines to link the pairs that go together.

face-to-face	appropriate
out of place	lying
telling the truth	without seeing the people we're talking to

🔑

6 Complete the following sentences with the correct phrases from Exercise 5.

a Before we go on, I need to know that you are ....

b Look, it would be much easier if we talked .... rather than on the phone.

c I feel really .... here. Can we go home? 🔑

●●● B Surviving an interview

1 Read this text about going for interviews.

home   support   contact us   terms and conditions

Let your body do the talking!

How to survive that interview, by Charlene Stewart

You're going for that all-important interview – for a place in a new school or college, or for a new job. You walk into the room and there they are – the interviewers – waiting to see what you are made of.

But did you know that the actual words you speak are less important than the way you look, the way you behave? Remember, they won't just be listening to you, they'll be watching you too, receiving all the messages you send out, consciously or unconsciously. And then they'll decide whether you are the right person for that place or that job.

NERVOUS? Don't be. Relax. Just follow our seven-point plan.

1 Don't cross anything! Keep arms, legs and feet relaxed and uncrossed. People with folded arms look like they're trying to protect themselves from something. They seem to be saying 'I am not confident.' If you're wearing a jacket, undo the buttons and open it up. An open jacket says 'I am an honest, open person. I have nothing to hide.'

2 Lean forward! Don't sit back. It makes you look tired or nervous. Sit forward, project yourself into the space. Show by the way you sit that you are ready and eager, that you want to be part of the scene.

3 Make direct eye contact! Avoid looking away all the time because it makes you look suspicious. Look directly at the people who are asking you questions or who you are talking to. If you lower your head all the time they won't be able to see the enthusiasm in your eyes.

4 Mirror their actions! One of the best ways of gaining people's trust and confidence is to move in the same way as they do. Listen to the speed at which they're talking, and watch the way they sit or move around. Do the same, but do it slowly at first. You don't want them to think you are making fun of them.

5 Go in confidently! A lot depends on how you enter the room. If you walk in nervously with your head and shoulders down, the interviewers won't think much of you from the outset. Go in with your head held high, a slight smile on your lips. When you shake hands with the interviewers don't be too enthusiastic, but make it strong and decisive. Nobody likes a weak handshake.

6 Use your head! When somebody asks you a question don't just say the first thing that comes into your head. Think about your answers. Always say to yourself, 'Why are they asking this question?' because when you know that, you'll probably be able to give an appropriate answer!

7 Think quickly! Studies have shown that people in interviews get most nervous when there is a silence. So be prepared to speak quickly and fluently. But use your head (see above).

Want to know more?
Enrol on one of our confidence courses. NOW!

2 Look back at the text on page 56. Circle the best ending to each of the following.

a The way you look and the body language you use are:

1 … as important as what you say.

2 … more important than what you say.

3 … not as important as what you say.

b It is important to:

1 … cross your legs.

2 … uncross your legs.

3 … look open and relaxed.

c In an interview you should:

1 … not look at the people asking questions.

2 … look directly at the people asking questions.

3 … look away when you are answering.

d At the beginning of an interview you should:

1 … show that you are confident.

2 … behave quietly and modestly.

3 … smile a lot.

e When you are asked a question you should:

1 … say to the interviewer 'Why are you asking this question?'

2 … think carefully but answer quickly.

3 … give yourself time to think carefully before answering, even if this involves silence.

3 Read the text again. Are the following statements *True* or *False* ?
Write T or F in the brackets.

a The web page is really an advertisement [ ] for a course or courses on how to survive interviews.

b Jackets should be kept undone in [ ] interviews.

c If you sit forward it shows that you [ ] are keen to get the job.

d Looking at interviewers makes them [ ] suspicious.

e Try out your interview in the mirror [ ] before you go in.

f A firm handshake is a good start to [ ] an interview.

g A quick answer to a question is more [ ] important than saying the right thing.

h You should try and understand what [ ] the interviewers are thinking.

i Silence makes people nervous. [ ]

4 Find words or phrases in the text that mean the opposite of the following.

a interviewee: ....

b consciously: ....

c become nervous or tense: ....

d crossed: ....

e sit back: ....

f unenthusiastic: ....

g raise: ....

h different: ....

i leave (a room): ....

j indecisive: ....

k not the right kind in the situation: ....

l leave (a course): ....

••• C Summarising reports

1 Read the following witness statement. It was written by the police officer who interviewed John Burney. The police officer wrote the statement in the first person (I = John Burney). John Burney will be asked to sign the statement. When you have read the statement, answer these questions.

a What crime took place? ....

b How many people were involved? ....

WITNESS STATEMENT FORM

NAME: John Burney
ADDRESS: 32 Albert Close, Glasgow GL2 1BT

STATEMENT

I was in the bank at 12.30. I saw two men and a girl run into the bank. A tall, white man with a gun ran up to the window and shouted something like 'Give me all your money.' He had short, dark hair. A second man, with a suitcase, went up to the window and helped the first man to put money into it. He was a 30-year-old, black man wearing jeans and a black sweater. He was very tall. The girl was about 25 with long blonde hair, wearing red trousers and a white shirt. When the suitcase was full I saw all three of them run out of the bank.

Signed: ....   Date: ....

---

2 Now read the transcript of what John Burney actually said (see below) and compare it with the witness statement written by the police officer.

Transcript of interview between Police Constable Davies and witness John Burney.

BURNEY:	There were two men, I think. No, three. They ran into the bank and the one with the gun, the tall one, he runs up to the what-do-you-call it, you know, where the cashier is, well, the window, anyway and starts shouting something, I don't know, 'Give me the money' or something. No, that was it, 'Give me all your money' and the other one –
POLICE OFFICER:	I thought you said there were three men?
BURNEY:	No, there were two men and a girl. It's the other man I'm talking about, the one carrying the suitcase, well, he goes up to the other guy –
POLICE OFFICER:	The one with the gun?
BURNEY:	Yes, and he opens the suitcase and the cashier, well, she – well, all the other people behind the window – they hand over piles of money and the two men put it into the suitcase and then they run out. It was 1.35. They had been in there for about 5 minutes.
POLICE OFFICER:	And the girl, what about the girl?
BURNEY:	Oh yeah, well, she just stands there keeping a lookout, I suppose, for the police – for you.
POLICE OFFICER:	Can you describe these people?
BURNEY:	Oh, yeah. The man with the gun was quite tall with long grey hair and dark glasses. The other one, the one with a suitcase, was a black guy, about one metre 70, one 75, probably about, you know, 30 years old, something like that. He was really skinny with jeans and a blue T-shirt.
POLICE OFFICER:	What about the girl?
BURNEY:	She had long blonde hair, you know, probably about 25 and really slim, with bright red trousers and a white shirt.

What three mistakes has the
police officer made?

a ....

....

b ....

....

c ....

....

3 Look at the picture. Write a conversation, like the one in Exercise 2,
between someone who saw the event and the police officer who is
interviewing them.

4 Using the conversation you have written, write a 'witness statement' like the one in Exercise 1.

•••A The case against computers

1 Write notes giving your opinion on the following questions.

Why do schools need computers? ....

....

What are computers most useful for? ....

....

2 Read the following text. Does the writer agree with you?

Wired? Not worth it!

Convinced that your kids will be left behind unless they become computer experts? Anxious that their school doesn't have enough computers? Well, don't be! Theodore Rosznak has 12 reasons why computers are definitely not a good idea.

1 Don't believe all the hype from the people who sell computers. They are just trying to sell more merchandise, and you can't always believe their claims.

2 People who say that schools need more computers are like doctors who prescribe medicine when the patient doesn't really need it.

3 By the time a school decides to buy a computer, it will be out of date. The manufacturers keep bringing out new models, and the old ones soon become outmoded.

4 The money schools use to buy computers could often be better spent on things that are more necessary – for example teachers' salaries, musical instruments or fixing the roof.

5 Whatever kids learn about computers in primary school, it won't be much use when they eventually get a job. Different firms have different computer systems, and employers should teach employees what they need to know after they hire them.

6 Computers don't create more jobs – they reduce the amount of work available. If we could get rid of computers right now, there would be many more jobs available for people to do!

7 Playing computer games is not the same as learning. Of course, games are fun – there's nothing wrong with that. But traditional learning teaches children many more important skills, such as concentrating for long periods of time, questioning things and developing memory.

8 As soon as you spend money on a computer, you will need to carry on spending just to keep up to date. (That's a lot of money down the drain!)

9 People who are computer enthusiasts often say that computers are educational, and rave about all the information the Internet can offer children. But beware if they tell you that information is everything. Information is only the answer to a question – it is the kind of question you ask that is important.

10 Learning isn't just about gathering information; it also means finding out about all kinds of ideas, values, tastes and opinions. Books offer the best ways of finding out about these things. Let your kids learn from all that authors and teachers have to offer.

11 The Internet is basically a huge advertising system. If a school asked for all advertising to be taken off the Internet, the manufacturers would tell them it was impossible. It isn't.

12 It is a myth that all children born since 1990 have an innate ability to use computers. Give a child a piece of paper and a pencil, and they will immediately draw or write something. But sit a young child in front of a computer, and he won't know where to begin!

3 Find which paragraph in the text says the opposite of the following statements. (Note down the paragraph number.) The first one has been done for you.

a A good computer system will last for a long time. ......**3**......

b Computer manufacturers are honest about what the machines do. ....

c Computers are better sources of information than books. ....

d Computer games help to teach children important skills. ....

e Schools always need more computers, just as a patient always needs medicine. ....

f School money is best spent on computers. ....

g Information is more important than asking the right questions. ....

h Most kids today find using computers easy. ....

i Once you've bought a computer system you won't have to spend any more money. ....

j Computers create jobs. ....

k Good computer skills learned in primary school will help children get a job when they grow up. ....

l The Internet doesn't have any advertisements on it. ....

4 Look at these words from the text. Tick the words you know.

hype ☐   myth ☐   prescribe ☐   kids ☐   enthusiasts ☐

wired ☐   salaries ☐   innate ☐   outmoded ☐

Use a dictionary to find out the meaning of any words you did not tick.

Language in chunks

5 Complete the following sentences using the phrases in the box.

> not a good idea   by the time   out of date   nothing wrong with that
> long periods of   down the drain   raves about

a .... you get home your dinner will be ready.

b Having another piece of cake is definitely .... You've had three pieces already.

c November 1999? These magazines are ....

d If you want to be a birdwatcher, expect .... boredom.

e Sue really likes that new American rock band. She .... the singer all the time!

f You want to buy a new computer? There's .... , except that you have got two already.

g I bought a new skirt last week, but it has split already. That's more money

....

6 Theodore Rosznak wrote this article in 1996. Is what it says still true, in your opinion?

B Loving technology

Star

Karen Chen is a film designer who has worked on films such as 'Beatrice', 'Trials and Efforts' and 'Romance in the Afternoon'. She tells Jane Markon about the gadgets in her life.

Are you a technophobe or technophile?

I'm definitely a technophile. I love technology because it saves me time and makes me money, so I use it all the time. My husband doesn't agree at all. He's a bit old-fashioned like that. I've only just managed to get him to buy his first mobile phone! But, as for me, I leave home at about 6.30 in the morning, after downloading emails on to my laptop. I deal with all my correspondence on my 55-minute journey to work – it's a good thing we live just near the train station. Then I do the same again – I download new emails before I leave work at about 5.15. It takes me the same time to get home, and by the time I get home I've finished for the day.

Which pieces of technology are important to you?

Three things: my Sharp laptop; my Nokia Communicator 9110I (mobile phone); and my Olympus Camedia Zoom (digital camera). I document everything: the kids, art, buildings, clothes, scenes that catch my eye as I walk past. My digicam has made taking photographs so much easier – and it's easier to send them to people. None of all that messy developing and printing!

What do you use your computer for?

Well, as I said, I send emails all the time. But I do a lot of my design work on screen now and I can send my ideas straight to directors and producers. I do a lot of research on the Internet too – there are some fantastic sites around now. You just type in www.google.com to start a search and you're off.

Who uses the computer at home?

The kids use the computer all the time at home. Of course they mail their friends endlessly – and on top of that they're always texting on their mobile phones! They play computer games when they think I or their father aren't looking! They do some of their homework on the computer too. They don't like doing homework, of course, but there are some really good revision sites on the Internet. I do a lot of my shopping on the net now – 15 minutes for a whole supermarket 'visit'! That feels really good. We book our holidays on the Internet too.

Which ISP do you use?

I have used various ISPs to connect me to my email and the Internet. The one I use at the moment is good because I just pay a monthly fee and there is no extra charge to my phone bill. The design of its site and systems is good – it's not too low-tech and not too high-tech.

Do you think email has changed the way we write?

Oh definitely. We use different language, don't we? And we write so much more quickly. I write things like 'c u at 6'. It's a pity we don't keep emails though. Can you imagine a book of letters between famous people being published in 50 years? I can't. But the good thing about emails is that people often send them instead of ringing you up and so you can decide when to answer them in your own time. It stops you being on demand. People can't just ring up and insist on speaking to you for hours.

What pieces of new technology do you think should be invented?

I want something that allows me to be working in my office and spending leisure time with my husband and children at the same time! I suppose that means a machine that can divide me into two!

1 Read the article opposite and then tick the statements about Karen Chen that are true.

a Karen Chen is married. ☐

b She leaves home at half past seven in the morning. ☐

c She travels to work by train. ☐

d She gets home at about ten past seven. ☐

e She is not interested in taking photographs. ☐

f She has written a book. ☐

g Homework is popular in Karen Chen's house. ☐

h Karen uses the Internet for shopping. ☐

i She prefers communicating by email than by phone. ☐

j Everyone in Karen's family loves technology. ☐ 🔑

2 Match the initials, words and phrases, most of which come from the text, with their meanings (in the box).

| a 'place' on the Internet that you can visit |
| a small computer you can carry with you |
| digital camera |
| Internet service provider |
| see you |
| technically complex |
| World Wide Web |
| technically simple |
| uniform resource locator (the address of a website or web page) |

a digicam: ....

b high-tech: ....

c ISP: ....

d laptop: ....

e low-tech: ....

f site: ....

g c u: ....

h URL: ....

i WWW: ....

🔑

3 Complete the following table with details about Karen.

a Journey time to and from work:	
b The place where Karen deals with correspondence:	
c The most important pieces of technology for Karen:	1
	2
	3
d What Karen and her family use the computer for:	1
	2
	3
	4
	5
	6
e The advantage of email:	🔑

●●● C txt msgng

The biggest growth in mobile phone use in the last five years has been text messaging. Users send written messages rather than leaving spoken ones. They use a special kind of language because they want to write quickly.

1 Match the text messages on the left with their meanings on the right. The first one has been done for you.

a 2DAY	all the best
b ATB	anyone
c B48	Are you OK?
d BCNU	by the way
e BTW	great
f CUL8R	lots of love
g GR8	love
h LOL	love and kisses
i LUV	no one
j NE1	Oh I see.
k NO1	See you later.
l OIC	someone
m RUOK	thanks
n SOME1	before eight
o THX	today
p WAN2	want to
q WKND	be seeing you
r XOXOXOXOX	weekend

a

Do U wan2 cum out with me?
Andy

b

Clown's Caf?
Andy

c

Fantastic! CU 2moro
Andy

d

Gr8!!!
Andy

e

O Pls. Just 1ns.
Andy

f

2moro? CU about 8?
Andy

g

OK. CU then.
Jill

h

No Thx.
Jill.

i

Where?
Jill

j

When?
Jill.

k

OK. Just 1ns.
Jill.

2 What do the text messages (a – k) mean? Can you translate them into ordinary English? Make a note of your answers in the spaces below.

a ....

b ....

c ....

d ....

e ....

f ....

g ....

h ....

i ....

j ....

k ....

Now put the messages in order. Andy's message (a) starts the sequence.

1 ...*a*...   2 ....   3 ....   4 ....   5 ....   6 ....

7 ....   8 ....   9 ....   10 ....   11 ....

3 Andy and Jill met up as a result of their text messages in Exercise 2. Write the text messages they sent each other the next day.

EXAMPLES:

Thx 4 lovely eve.
CU on Tuesday.

Jill XXX

Sorry about what I said.
Can I CU L8TR?

Andy

●●●A Who wrote Shakespeare?

1 Read the article that follows and then note down the connection between William Shakespeare and the following:

a Stratford-upon-Avon ....

d education ....

b Romeo and Juliet ....

e handwritten manuscripts ....

c films ....

f the Earl of Oxford ....

The great Shakespeare controversy:
who really wrote Romeo and Juliet?

William Shakespeare, England's greatest writer, was responsible for 39 plays and some of the most fantastic poetry ever written. He was born in Stratford-upon-Avon on 23 April 1564. Later he went to London where he wrote, and acted in, plays such as Romeo and Juliet, Macbeth, Hamlet and The Tempest. He died in Stratford in 1616, but films are still being made about him and his work 400 years later.

However, some people don't believe that William Shakespeare of Stratford could have written the plays. They say that he wasn't educated well enough to know about all the things mentioned in the plays. Besides, there are no manuscripts in Shakespeare's handwriting, and his name didn't even appear on many of his plays until after his death.

One group of people argue that the plays must have been written by Edward de Vere, the Earl of Oxford. He wasn't allowed to use his own name, because he was an aristocrat, and so he chose 'Shakespeare' as a pseudonym.

2 Are the following statements *True* or *False*? Write T or F in the brackets.

a A man called William Shakespeare came   [ ]
  from Stratford-upon-Avon.

b The Avon is a river.   [ ]

c William Shakespeare was very well educated. [ ]

d People wrote plays and books (manuscripts) [ ]
  by hand in Shakespeare's day.

e The Earl of Oxford was a farm labourer.   [ ]

f A pseudonym is a name a person uses   [ ]
  instead of their real name.

3 Put the following emails between Luke and Hannah in the correct order. A is the first one in the sequence.

A
Dear Hannah,
Thanks for your mail.
You ask why I think the Earl of Oxford wrote 'Shakespeare's' plays? Well, to start with William Shakespeare of Stratford was uneducated. He didn't go to university or anything. He never travelled. How could he have known all the history in the plays? For example, how did he know all about Italy, where Romeo and Juliet takes place?
Love
Luke

B
Dear Luke,
No writer put their name on their plays in the 1580s and '90s! It just wasn't the custom. But in the first complete collection of all the plays (published in 1623, after Shakespeare's death) Shakespeare is described as the 'sweet swan of Avon'. The River Avon runs through Stratford-upon-Avon. So he must have been talking about William Shakespeare from Stratford.
OK?
Hannah

C
Yes, but the Earl of Oxford had an estate in Bilton – and that had a different River Avon near it. The 'swan of Avon' might have been the swan of BILTON-upon-Avon – in other words, the Earl of Oxford.
What do you have to say about that?
Luke

D
Oh, come on, Luke! Don't repeat that old Oxford Avon story! The Earl of Oxford sold his estate at Bilton in 1580 – and nobody called Shakespeare the 'swan of Avon' until 1623!
Be logical :-)
Hannah.

E
Ah yes, Hannah, but that's the question. Who was he?
Luke
BTW why don't you have a look at the Shakespeare Oxford Society website? http://www.shakespeare-oxford.com

F
Does it matter if I can't prove anything? You can't either. You keep talking about who Shakespeare must have been – he must have been an aristocrat, he must have been educated, he must have been this, he must have been that. But all that matters to me is who he really was.
H.

G
Hannah,
Self-taught Shakespeare! That just can't have happened! Anyway, how come his name wasn't on any of his plays?
Luke

H
Dear Luke,
OK, so perhaps Shakespeare wasn't educated. But his neighbour in Stratford was John Field, who published books – Shakespeare could have read those books to get information about foreign countries and English history. He might have read those. He was probably self-taught.
Best wishes,
Hannah

I
Hi Hannah,
'Logical'! You're joking, surely? You'll never be able to prove that the Avon in the 1623 edition of the plays was the Stratford Avon. It could have been a different river, the River Avon at Bilton – whether the Earl of Oxford sold it or not. Let's face it, you can't prove anything about Shakespeare, can you?
Luke.

1 _A_ 2 .... 3 .... 4 .... 5 .... 6 .... 7 .... 8 .... 9 ....

....

4 Answer the following questions.

a Who was John Field and where did he live? ....

b Who was described as the 'sweet swan of Avon'? ....

c How many River Avons do Luke and Hannah talk about? Where are they? ....

d When was the first complete collection of Shakespeare plays published? ....

e When did the Earl of Oxford sell his estate at Bilton? ....

●●● B All I want

1 Read this introduction and then write down the names that go with the descriptions (a–e).

All I Want, by Margaret Johnson, tells the story of Alex Faye. Alex works in an art gallery. She started the job three weeks ago.

The gallery is in trouble because it sold paintings by an artist called Ralph Blackman – except that they weren't by Ralph Blackman at all, so everyone is very embarrassed by the mistake.

Alex is crazy about her boss, Brad Courtenay. She thinks she's in love with him. Brad is the owner of the gallery. He has taken her to his house.

a The writer of the book: ....

....

b The central character (who works in an art gallery): ....

c He owns the art gallery: ....

....

d He's a painter: ....

e The person Alex is in love with: ....

2 Read the extract below from *All I Want*. Match the lines (a–f) with the numbers in the text. Note the correct numbers in the brackets.

a Do you like them?   [   ]

b It's not a snow scene.   [   ]

c Just … just not modern art.   [   ]

d Name three paintings by Van Gogh.   [   ]

e Of course I like them!   [   ]

f Oh, what a fantastic view!   [   ]

This is the studio,' he says, leading the way into a big square room with very large windows.

'(1) ....' I say, crossing to the window to look out. Outside the skies are still dark, but it hasn't started to rain yet. But even in this poor light the view of File Beacon is wonderful. The room is perfect for an artist.

Brad doesn't seem interested in the view. I can hear him moving things around in the room behind me, and when I turn round I notice several paintings leaning against the wall. They're facing the wrong way, but because of the view from the window, I guess they will be landscapes. I'm so sure about it that when Brad turns two round the right way, I can't help but gasp in surprise.

'What is it?' he asks, frowning at me.

'(2) .... '

For a moment I can't think of anything to say. The paintings aren't landscapes at all. To be honest, I've no idea *what* they are. One of them seems to be completely black except for a small green spot in one corner, and the other seems to be all white. All white. It doesn't even have any spots.

'Yes!' I cry quickly. '(3) .... They're …'. But I have to stop because I can't think of how to continue the sentence. Panicking a little, I start another one. 'Is … is that one a snow scene?' I ask.

My question is followed by a long silence. It's as quiet as it was in the gallery office. I can hear his breathing again. I realise I've made a big mistake.

'No, Alex,' he says at last, '(4) .... It's not a scene at all. I'm not a landscape painter.'

'Oh,' I say swallowing nervously. 'Sorry. I … I don't know much about modern art.'

'So it would seem.' Brad returns his paintings to their place against the wall as if I'm no longer allowed to see them. 'And yet, if I remember correctly, when you came to the job interview, you told me you knew a lot about art.'

It's true. I did say that. OK, I lied. But you see, as soon as I saw Brad, I knew I had to get the job. I was a desperate girl and I took desperate action.

'I ... well, I do know about art,' I say. 'Well, a bit, anyway. (5) '.................................... !'

'OK. Who's your favourite artist?' he demands to know.

By now I'm panicking so much that for the moment the only artist's name I can remember is Ralph Blackman's. Luckily I realise it wouldn't be a good idea to say his name, though, and I think for a little while longer.

'Van Gogh!' I shout at last, and he looks at me doubtfully.

'OK,' he says. '(6) .... !'

'Umm ...,' I say, thinking hard.

'Two paintings.'

'Umm ...'

'Come on Alex! *One* painting.'

Suddenly I remember one, and shout out its name excitedly. 'Sunflowers!'

Brad doesn't seem to be impressed. He shakes his head. 'Alex, every person in the world has heard of Sunflowers,' he says.

'Well I haven't got a very good memory for names,' I say weakly. 'That's why I can't think of any more titles.'

3 Are the following statements *True* or *False*? Write T or F in the brackets.

a In the extract 'I' is Alex.   [   ]

b It's probably going to rain soon.   [   ]

c When she goes into the room Alex sees the back of some   [   ]
   pictures.

d Alex thinks the paintings will be pictures of the   [   ]
   countryside.

e One painting is white with a green spot.   [   ]

f Brad paints pictures of the countryside.   [   ]

g Alex likes Brad's pictures.   [   ]

h Alex always tells the truth.   [   ]

i Alex knows a lot about art.   [   ]

j Alex met Brad for the first time at her interview.   [   ]

k 'Sunflowers' was painted by Van Gogh.   [   ] 🔑

4 Is Brad going to fall in love with Alex, do you think? Write a paragraph explaining your answer.

....

....

....

....

....

....

....

....

●●● C First lines

1 What does the first line of a story or a novel have to do? Choose one or more of the following.

- be exciting
- be funny
- be mysterious
- describe a character
- describe a place
- give information

2 Here are some first lines from published novels. Which one makes you want to go on and read the rest of the book?

1 All this happened, more or less.

2 Many years later as he faced the firing squad, Colonel Aureliano Buendia was to remember that distant afternoon when his father took him to discover ice.

3 Polly Alter used to like men, but she didn't trust them any more, or have very much to do with them.

4 The place I like best in this world is the kitchen.

5 There was a death at its beginning as there would be a death again at its end.

6 'You too will marry a boy I choose,' said Mrs Rupa Mehra firmly to her younger daughter.

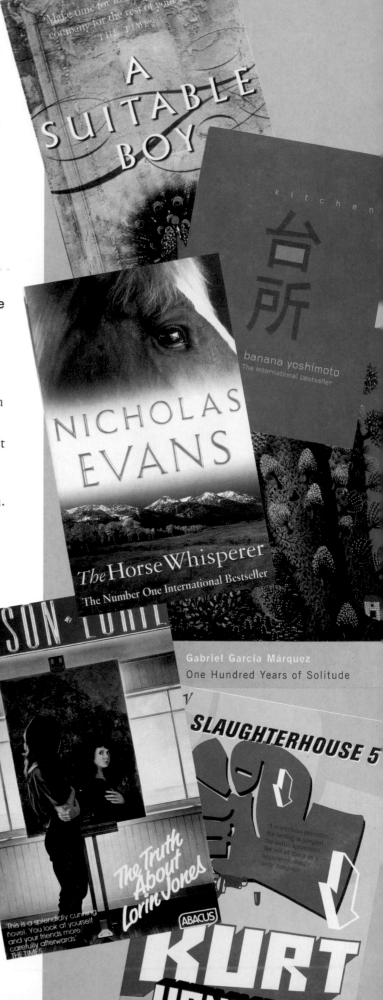

3 Now read the following book descriptions and write in the brackets which of the first lines in Exercise 2 comes from which book.

a *A Suitable Boy* by Vikram Seth. A huge novel about a young girl's search for love – and a husband. Set in India, it presents a panoramic view of a whole nation, and offers a unique insight into the human heart.   [   ]

b *The Horse Whisperer* by Nicholas Evans. After a horrific horse-riding accident a young girl is terribly injured – both physically and mentally. Her horse has also been hurt and the girl's mother takes both girl and horse to an expert for help. A moving tale of love and suffering.   [   ]

c *Kitchen* by Banana Yoshimoto. The setting is contemporary Japan, where a pair of young women discover the meaning of life. The writing may be simple, but the words stay in the mind long after the book is closed.   [   ]

d *One Hundred Years of Solitude* by Gabriel Garcia Marquez. A classic of twentieth-century Latin American literature, this novel charts a century of fantastical happenings in the imaginary South American town of Macondo.   [   ]

e *Slaughterhouse 5* by Kurt Vonnegut. One of the most original anti-war novels ever written. Billy Pilgrim, a prisoner of war, witnesses the fire-bombing of Dresden, one of the most destructive acts of the twentieth century. Miraculous, bitter and funny.   [   ]

f *The Truth about Lorin Jones* by Alison Lurie. A feminist art historian sets out to rescue the reputation of an artist and to discover the truth about her life. But she finds out more than she expected – especially about herself.   [   ]

4 Choose a topic from the box below.

a power cut

looking for water in the desert

a beauty contest

a disastrous driving test

a wedding

a Write the first sentence of your story about the topic you have chosen.

....

....

....

b Think about the sentence you have written. What could follow it? Write the second sentence.

....

....

....

c Write the next three sentences, always looking back at what you have written in previous sentences.

....

....

....

....

....

....

If you can, show your story to someone who speaks English. Do they want to go on and read the rest of 'your book'?

●●● A In the manager's office

1 Read the text below. Where do you think the text comes from. Is it from:

a ... *Football Manager* (a magazine for anyone interested in running a football club)?
b ... the sports pages of a newspaper?
c ... a novel called *The Manager's Dilemma*?
d ... *Management Today* (a magazine for business people)?

THE MANAGER'S OFFICE

When Paul walked into the manager's office he knew something was wrong. Bob didn't say hello in the usual way. He didn't even look up from his desk. Paul stood there awkwardly wondering whether to shut the door.

Two minutes passed.

'Bob,' he said nervously, 'is something the matter?'

'You tell me,' he replied, looking at him intently, with no trace of a smile. He realised that he was angry about something.

'Look,' he stammered, '(1) .... Or do you want me to just stand here?'

Bob took off his glasses and stood up. He stretched, turned his back on the other man and walked to the large plate glass window at one side of the room.

'(2) ....,' he said, so quietly that Paul could hardly hear his voice.

'What do you mean?' He hadn't expected this. 'I am "in shape" as you call it.'

'Are you? Are you really? I don't think so. You've been missing training sessions, and I think you're unfit and – on top of that –' Bob picked up that morning's newspaper, 'I have to read about you in the Daily Mirror.

Look at this!' he almost shouted at him, 'What on earth were you thinking of?'

'(3) ....'

'There's nothing to explain, Paul. You're out every evening at parties having a good time with your friends. God knows what you get up to. I've had enough of it.' He turned to face him. 'Frankly, Paul, I think I've had enough of you.'

'(4) ....'

'You'd what, Paul? Leave the club? Complain to the manager? But that's just the problem for you isn't it? I am the manager.'

'Look, Bob, I'm sorry; honestly I am.' He walked over to stand beside him. From here you could see right into the stadium. Some of his team-mates were down there kicking balls around. He should be with them. He knew that. But he'd got up late and he felt terrible.

'(5) ....' There. He had said it.

'You can't mean that.'

'Oh but I do, Paul, I do. Just because we have the same mother and father ... .'

'Brothers Bob! We're brothers. Go on, say it, I know it's difficult for you. You've always hated the fact that I'm a great footballer, better than you could ever be. Sometimes I wonder how we can exist in the same club ...'.

'That makes two of us, Paul.'

The silence in the room grew louder. Paul didn't know what to say or do. It was true that he had missed a lot of training sessions. It was true he was going out a lot. But that's because everyone asked him to. He was one of the most famous players in the world. The newspapers wanted photographs of him all the time. People wanted to talk to him. They wanted to get to know him. Anyway, he enjoyed going out, he liked the attention. As for the team, the club ...

'So tell me,' Bob said, interrupting his thoughts, 'how important is the game to you? How much do you want to play?'

Paul's brother must have read his thoughts. What could he say to him now?

2 Read the following lines of conversation. They have been taken out of the text. Write in the brackets the number of the space that each has been taken from.

a If I thought you meant that, I'd …   [   ]
b If I've done anything to offend you, anything at all, please tell me. [   ]
c If you don't change your ways, you'll be out of the team.   [   ]
d If you don't get in shape soon, I'll have to let you go.   [   ]
e If you'd just let me explain …   [   ]

3 Answer the following questions.

a Who is the player? ....

b Who is the manager? ....

c What is the game? ....

d Why is the manager angry with the player? Give three reasons.

　　1 ....

　　2 ....

　　3 ....

e What is the relationship between the manager and the player? ....

4 Find words or phrases in the text with the following meanings. The first letter of each word is given.

a with a feeling of embarrassment, not knowing what to say: a.........................

b to speak with pauses and repeated sounds because you are nervous: s.........................

c to straighten your arms, back, etc. for relaxation: s.........................

d almost not: h.........................

e times when teams practice to get fit (two words): t................. s.................

f popular at a particular time: f.........................

g to do something a little bit bad or wicked (three words): g............. u............. t............. something

h a large building for football matches, with a pitch and seats: s.........................

Language in chunks

5 Complete the following phrases using words from the text. The meanings are given in brackets. The first one has been done for you.

a he ....*turned his back*.... on the other man (he turned round, away from him)

b if you don't .... soon (become fit)

c I've .... you (it has been too much for me)

d if you don't .... (behave differently)

e That .... (I feel exactly the same as you)

f .... his thoughts (stopping him thinking)

g he must have .... (guessed what he was thinking)

•••B The women of Fulham LFC

1 Read the text that follows and then answer the questions. Who:

a ... scored 19 goals? ....

b ... only scored one goal? ....

c ... is the youngest player in Fulham Ladies Football Club? ....

d ... is about to get a doctorate in computer science? ....

e ... has played for the Indian national football team? ....

f ... plays for England? ....

g ... obviously weren't interested in football? ....

h ... thinks it's good that Rachel trains young people? ....

i ... shouted comments that weren't funny? ....

Not just a man's game

Stephanie Merritt meets the young women of Fulham LFC

Photographs by Lina Ahnoff

A damp cold day in February. I watch as two football teams walk off the pitch after a game. The players from the Stowmarket team look exhausted, red-faced, and very very unhappy. Well, you can understand it. They have just lost their game 19-1.

Welcome to the world of women's football! The team that beat Stowmarket is Fulham LFC, the only fully professional women's side in Britain.

Fulham LFC has players of all ages, from 17-year-old Chantelle White to Permi Jhooti, a 30-year-old who has not only played for the Indian national women's team, but is also just finishing her doctorate in computer science. 'If I'm lucky,' she says, 'I'll be able to play for another five years. I do have another occupation, though, and that's what I'll be doing for the rest of my life. But right now I can do what I really love — football — just for a bit longer. I'm really lucky.'

All the players in the team talk about how difficult it was to find female role models in the sport. 'When we were younger it was really hard because there were no women footballers to look up to and admire,' says 21-year-old Rachel Yankey. 'It was definitely seen as a boy's game, and the only well-known players were men. We're trying to change that, to help young girls who want to play football to see that it's not just a man's game.'

That's why, on a cold rainy Monday afternoon, I find myself at a state school in West London. Rachel is training a group of youngsters. They are typical teenagers: the two who are using their mobile phones to send text messages probably won't play for England when they are older, but some of them are really enthusiastic.

'It's really good for girls to be trained by Rachel,' says Clinton Joseph a youth sport coordinator. 'She's a London girl and the kids here see her as a big sister. They know she plays for England, and that sounds pretty good to some of them.'

What do men think of women playing football? 'A lot of the time when you meet blokes and tell them you're a professional footballer they don't believe you,' Chantelle White, 17, explains, 'but when they come and watch us play they're all really surprised at how good we are.' She obviously hasn't encountered the middle-aged man who sat behind me during one match I went to. He was shouting comments that he thought were funny. For example, when the game stopped for injury (something that happens all the time in men's football), he yelled 'What's up ref — does she need to do her hair?' How depressing! This, I thought, was typical male behaviour. But then I looked at the other men around me. They had heard the middle-aged man too but they weren't laughing. None of them thought he was funny at all. Just a sad, old voice from an earlier time.

Women's football isn't a joke any more, even if it ever was. And if you don't believe me, go and watch Chantelle, Rachel, Permi and their team-mates on any Saturday during the season. They're an inspiring sight.

2 **Look at the way the following words and phrases are used in the text and then write them in the correct gaps (a–k) below.**

blokes
coordinator
damp
enthusiastic
inspiring
look up to
professional
ref
role model
side
typical

a When the weather is slightly wet we can say that it is ....

b When someone does a sport for money (rather than just as a hobby) we say they are a ....

c A .... is someone who you try and imitate because you admire them.

d We .... people we admire and respect.

e Someone who is .... is very keen on and involved in something.

f .... is a slang word for 'men'.

g Footballers and football supporters often call the referee '........................' .

h Another word for a 'team' in a game is a ....

i Someone who organises different parts of an activity and brings things together is a ....

j Something that is just as you would expect it to be is referred to as ....

k Something that is very good, and makes you want to do better is ....

3 **Complete the following sentences about the text.**

a We know that Fulham LFC is special because ....

b We know what Permi thinks of football because ....

c We know that players like Rachel had trouble when they started because ....

d We know that some of the students with Rachel weren't interested in football because ....

e We know other men didn't think the middle-aged man was funny because ....

●●● C Using acronyms

1 Read the article that follows and, in the brackets, note down the picture number that goes with each paragraph.

Dealing with a sports injury

If you hurt yourself, stop immediately. If the injury seems minor, follow the **RICE** principles.

R is for Rest. Give painful muscles plenty of time to recover if you want to avoid serious damage. If it hurts, avoid exercise until you can gently begin again. If the injury is less serious, you can do 'active rest', which means gently exercising the area until it is back to its former strength and full range of movement. Pain is the guide – if it really hurts, seek medical attention. [ ]

I is for Ice. Apply using an ice pack or even a bag of frozen peas wrapped in a towel. Keep it on the sprain or strain for 15 minutes and repeat several times in the first 48 hours. If the swelling and pain do not disappear, seek medical help. Don't apply heat, because this increases the blood circulation and swelling in damaged areas. [ ]

C is for Compress. A bandage or elastic support worn over the injury will help stop bleeding and reduce the swelling. But it won't work if the compress is too tight or too loose. [ ]

E is for Elevate. If it is a minor injury (particularly in the case of the knee, foot or ankle), resting and raising the leg by more than 20 or 30 degrees above hip level within 24 hours of the injury will prevent or reduce swelling. [ ]

NB: **RICE** is a recognised acronym used by chartered physiotherapists.

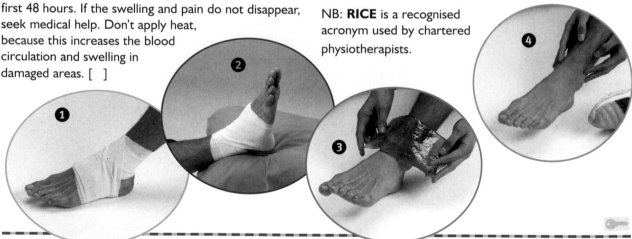

2 Explain the importance of the following in the RICE principles?

a pain: ....

b a bag of frozen peas: ....

c a towel: ....

d heat: ....

e a bandage: ....

f hip level: ....

3 Look at the following dictionary definition of the word 'acronym'.

acronym: a word made up of the first letters of other words

Join phrases from the two columns below to make names. What are the acronyms?

Self-Contained	by Stimulated Emission of Radiation	a ....
Light Amplification	Educational Scientific and Cultural Organisation	b ....
North Atlantic	Tax	c ....
United Nations	Treaty Organization	d ....
Value Added	Underwater Breathing Apparatus	e ....

- -

4 Make up an acronym to help people to remember what to do in a particular situation. Describe what each letter in your acronym stands for. You can choose one of the following situations or invent one of your own.

- Having people for dinner
- Using a technical device (e.g. a computer program, a mobile phone)
- Planning a journey/holiday
- Preparing for an exam
- Having a party

Here is an example:

Having people for dinner

M *eet ... your guests with a smile on your face.*
E *ntertain ... your guests and make sure they talk to each other.*
A *greement ... is better than argument around the dinner table.*
L *eave ... the washing up until afterwards.*

....

....

....

....

....

....

....

....

....

●●● A The cellist

1 Read the text below and then answer the questions that follow it.

There was only one chair on the stage of the concert hall in northern England. There was no piano, no music stand and no conductor. Just that solitary chair.

The atmosphere in the hall was tense. People were nervous and excited. Everyone in the audience of 600 people knew that they were going to hear a very special kind of music.

Finally it was time to start. Yo-Yo Ma, one of the world's most famous cellists, came on to the stage, bowed to the audience and sat down quietly on the chair. He made himself comfortable, thought for some minutes until there was complete silence, and then he started to play music that was at first empty and dangerous, but that soon became loud and painful, like the worst thing you've ever heard. It was almost unbearable but then, finally, it faded away to nothing. Yo-Yo Ma did not move. He stayed with his head bowed over his instrument.

Everyone in the hall held their breath. For what seemed like hours, nobody moved. It was as if they had all experienced something terrible and dark.

But then Yo-Yo Ma stood up. He put down his cello. He stretched out his hand to someone in the audience, asking them to come and join him. An electric shock ran through the audience when they realised what was going to happen.

A man got up from his seat and walked towards the stage. He was dressed in dirty motorcycle leathers, but Ma did not seem to mind. He rushed down from the stage, and when the two men met they flung their arms around each other in an emotional embrace.

The audience went crazy; suddenly everyone was cheering and shouting, like people do when they've just heard great music. But this was more than music.

a Who played at the concert? ....

b How many people were in the audience? ....

c What was the music like? ....

....

d How did the audience react as the music finished? ....

....

e What happened next? ....

f How did the audience react then? ....

....

2 Complete the table below using words from the text.

a Words about musical instruments, musical furniture, and musicians:	b Adjectives describing how people feel:	c Adjectives describing something bad:

Tick the words you know. Use your dictionary to look up the words you do not know.

Language in chunks

3 Explain the meaning of the phrases in italics, which are taken from the text.

a He *made himself comfortable*. ....

b There was *complete silence*. ....

c Everyone *held their breath*. ....

d They *flung their arms around each other*. ....

e The audience *went crazy*. ....

4 Use the phrases from Exercise 3 to answer the following questions. You may have to change the tense of the verbs and some other words.

a What do you do when you swim underwater?..

b What do you do at the start of a long rail journey? ....

c What might you hear in the middle of the Arctic or Antarctic? ....

d What would you and your best friend do if you met after not seeing each other for a long time?

....

e What would you do at the end of a concert by your favourite musician?....................

5 Think about the following questions.

a Why does the text say 'this was more than music'.

b What do you think is the connection between the music, Yo-Yo Ma and the man dressed in motorcycle leathers?

By reading texts 1–3 in the next section (Section B) you will find out the answers.

●●● B The story of Vedran Smailovic

(Before working on this section, make sure you have read the text in the previous section (Section A).)

1 Read Text 1 and then answer the questions.

TEXT 1

In the early 1990s, there was a terrible war in Yugoslavia. Many people died, both soldiers and civilians. The city of Sarajevo was for many months one of the most dangerous places in the world. It was constantly under attack and its civilian inhabitants had to live with no electricity and little water. Only a few shops stayed open to sell food.

On 27 May 1992, one of the shops, a bakery, opened in the afternoon and a long line of men, women and children queued to buy fresh bread. But it was not to be. At four o'clock a mortar shell exploded in the street and 22 innocent people were killed.

A man called Vedran Smailovic lived near the scene of this terrible tragedy. He was 35 at the time, and when he heard the news he decided to do something about it.

a Why was there a queue of people in the street on 27 May 1992? ....

....

b What happened at four o'clock? ....

....

c How many people died? ....

d When exactly did they die? ....

e Who were they? ....

....

f Who is or was Vedran Smailovic? ....

....

2 Read Text 2 and then answer the questions.

TEXT 2

Before the war, Vedran Smailovic had been a cellist with the Sarajevo Opera. When he heard about an explosion that had killed men, women and children in a bread queue in Sarajevo, he decided to do something about it. And so he did what he did best. He played his cello.

For the next 22 days at exactly four o'clock in the afternoon he put on his concert clothes, took his cello and a plastic chair into the empty streets and played a piece of music by the composer Albinoni – his Adagio in G Minor, one of the saddest pieces of music ever. Around him there was fighting and death. Shells fell and bullets flew while he played, but he was never hurt. With the world collapsing around him he played for compassion and peace, to ease the pain of loss and to preserve the dignity of the human race.

a What was Vedran Smailovic's job before the war? ....

....

b What did Vedran Smailovic decide to do when he heard the news and how did he do it?

....

....

c What piece of music did he play? ....

....

d Why did he play his cello? ....

....

....

e Was he ever hurt? ....

....

3 Read Text 3 and then answer the questions.

TEXT 3

David Wilde, an English composer, read a story in his newspaper that moved him deeply. It was about a man called Vedran Smailovic, who played his cello in the street in the middle of a war to honour the dead. His courage was extraordinary because he sat in the street and played while shells and bullets flew around him.

David Wilde was so inspired by the story that he wrote a special piece for solo cello, which he called *The Cellist of Sarajevo*. It was performed by the cellist Yo-Yo Ma at the Manchester cello festival in April 1994. Incredibly, Vedran Smailovic had survived the war and was in the audience that night to hear it. When Yo-Yo Ma finished playing, the two men embraced in front of a cheering audience.

a Who is David Wilde? ....

....

b What did he read about? ....

....

c What did he do then? ....

....

d Where was *The Cellist of Sarajevo* performed?

....

e Who played it? ....

f Who was in the audience? ....

....

4 Based on the information in the text in Section A and in Texts 1–3 above, answer these questions.

a What was the piece of music in the concert called? ....

....

b Who wrote it? ....

c Why did he write it? ....

....

d What had Vedran Smailovic done and why? ....

....

....

e Who was the man in the audience wearing motorcycle leathers? ....

....

5 What words would you choose from the following lists to describe Vedran Smailovic's action? What other words could you use?

- beautiful
- brave
- dramatic
- gentle
- ....
- ....
- ....

- foolish
- irresponsible
- useless
- crazy
- ....
- ....
- ....

●●● C Correcting and ordering

1 Read the following corrected piece of homework by an elementary student, and then complete the 'correction symbols' chart with the correct symbols.

Music is my fav<u>e</u>rite thing. [SP] I like <u>very much it</u>. [WO] I have <u>learned</u> [t] the piano when I was young but now I don't [to] play very much at all.

My sister pla<u>y</u> [C] in a rock band. She is very keen / heavy metal music, though I don't like it at all because I <u>am better in</u> [WW] jazz-style music.

My friend <u>p</u>eter [P] lik<u>e</u> [C] heavy metal music too. He has a lot of <u>informations</u> [g] about it – and he also likes <u>a lot my sister</u>! [WO]

CORRECTION SYMBOLS

Symbol	Meaning
a	Something has been left out.
b	Something that is not necessary has been put in.
c	There is a spelling mistake.
d	The student has used the wrong word(s).
e	There is a grammar mistake.
f	The verb doesn't agree with its subject – 'concord'.
g	There is a punctuation mistake.
h	The verb tense is wrong.
i	The word order is wrong.

2 Write a correct version of the student's composition in Exercise 1.

3 Look at the following statement.

All children should learn a musical instrument at school.

Do you agree with it?

. . . .

4 Read the following opinions. What do you think?
Write A (= *Agree*) or D (= *Disagree*) in the brackets.

a Music can be enjoyed all your life.   [   ]

b Children take pride in progress.   [   ]

c Children develop intellectually if they learn an instrument.   [   ]

d Instruments are expensive to buy or hire.   [   ]

e Not everyone likes music.   [   ]

f There's nothing special about music.   [   ]

g Other subjects (e.g. maths, science) are more important.   [   ]

h Playing in music groups is good for cooperation.   [   ]

i Practising a musical instrument is good for self-discipline.   [   ]

j Instrumental playing helps mind and body coordination.   [   ]

k Some children are bored by music.   [   ]

l Some children have no musical talent.   [   ]

Now list the opinions (a–l) in the correct columns below.

For (in favour of) learning a musical instrument   Against learning a music instrument

. . . .

5 Use some of the opinions from Exercise 4 to write one paragraph of
not more than four sentences, either in favour of or against the
statement in Exercise 3 above.

....

....

....

....

....

....

....

UNIT 14

●●● A Rachel

1 Read the text. It comes from a book called *Trumpet Voluntary*. Do you think the book is:

a … an instruction book for trumpet players?

b … a story of romantic love?

c … a study of one of the most famous pieces of 17th century music?

I liked Rachel. She was quiet and gentle. She had light brown hair, and pretty brown eyes set in a round, pleasant face. When she smiled she looked like a happy child and you knew you could trust her. She was very easy to talk to.

That night we sat and talked about what we hoped for in the future. I told her I wanted to make enough money as a musician to have a nice house, travel a bit, that kind of thing. She told me that her dreams were much the same. She wanted children one day, she said, but for that she'd need to find the right man.

'Well it's no good looking at me,' I said, as a joke.

'I know that, you fool,' she said, laughing at me. 'You can't see anybody anyway. Not while Malgosia is in the way.' I blushed.

'Maybe,' I replied. I didn't like talking about it.

'Can I say something?' Rachel asked, nervously.

'It depends what it is,' I replied. Around us people were talking and laughing as the night got darker. I saw the lights of a party boat travelling along the river in front of us.

'It's just that, well, I know Malgosia is beautiful. I mean really beautiful. I wish I was beautiful like that. And I do like her. But she's crazy about Tibor, and anyone who's crazy about Tibor, well …'. She stopped and looked at me, wondering how I would react.

'Well what?' I answered. I understood what she was saying, I think, but I didn't like anyone criticising Malgosia.

'Oh, now you're cross with me,' Rachel worried. 'Sorry. Sorry. But it's just a pity to see you and her. She's not right for you. You're wasting your time, wasting your life on her and you're not getting anything back. It doesn't look good. That's what I think.'

'Well,' I snapped back, without thinking, 'I don't care what you think, OK? Me and Malgosia, well, we're …'. I wanted a word that meant more than 'friend' but I couldn't think of the right one – 'we're special, all right? So it's none of your business. Just keep out of my affairs, OK?'

Rachel had gone red and I had gone too far. My only excuse is that I was very confused then, and still very young. But I suppose, if I am honest, that wasn't it. It was because Rachel had said something that I didn't want to hear because it was the truth. Now I think that if only I had listened to her then, if only I had understood what she was trying to tell me, I might not have made the decisions that I did and my life might have turned out very differently.

2 Find words or phrases in the text with the following meanings. The first letter is given for each.

a a stupid person: f..

b to go red from embarrassment: b ....

c to be really in love with someone: c..........................

    a...

d to say/do something because of what someone

    else has said/done: r.......................................

e saying bad things about someone: c..........................

f angry: c..................................

g to say something suddenly because you are

    angry: s...

3 Read the text again. What do you know about the following people?

a the narrator: ....

    ....

b Rachel: ....

    ....

c Tibor: ....

d Malgosia: ....

4 Without looking back at the text, rewrite the following with the correct punctuation.

a can I say something Rachel asked nervously

b I know that you fool she said laughing at me

c well what I answered

Language in chunks

5 Complete these phrases from the text and explain what they mean.

a She was very easy .... = ...

b She's not .... = ...

c You're wasting .... = ...

d I don't care what .... = ...

e It's none of .... = ...

f Keep out of .... = ...

g I had gone .... = ...

Which two phrases are used in an aggressive way?

....

6 The narrator says, 'If only I had listened to her then … my life might have turned out very differently.' What do you think he means? What do you think happened to him?

●● B How do you know it's love?

1 Read the following statements. Tick the first column if you agree with them.

a Being attracted to someone isn't the same as being in love with them.			
b It's difficult to say whether 'this is love'.			1
c Some people think they are in love, but actually they just don't want to be alone.			
d There are many different kinds of love.			
e When you love someone you feel as if they are with you even when you are apart.			
f When you love someone you want to be with them.			
g When you love someone you want to share everything with them.			
h You can't love someone unless you love yourself.			
i You know whether or not you are in love.			

2 Now read the text below. In what order do the points occur in the text? Write in the numbers in the second column above. The first one has been done for you.

welcome • site index • daily updates

Channels
advice

love library

romance

dating guide

dining

online love

holidays

gift shop

Is This Love? A Closer Look
by Bob Narindra

One of the most common questions we get asked at Lovingyou.com is 'How do you know if it is really love?' Well, as you can imagine, this also happens to be one of the most difficult questions to answer! Love is such a strange, wonderful thing that nobody really understands what it is yet. Another problem is that there are so many different kinds of love: the love you feel for a friend, a family member, a sport or even a pet. Love is such a crazy emotion that there is absolutely no way that I can definitively answer how you know when it is love … but I am going to give it a try!

Now, in order to find out if you love someone, the basic place to start would be to ask yourself, do you want to be with them. If the answer to that question is no, then it really can't be love. When you love someone, you want to be with them. Not just be with them, but share everything with them. You have a great day at work and want to rush home and tell them every wonderful thing that has happened. You feel excited at the prospect of just being in their company; just being close to them isn't enough, you want to be a part of them, a part of their life forever. You can't stand the thought of being away from them but, when you are, you still feel that bond that ties you together wherever you go. You can almost feel what they are feeling. You feel like, with a little bit of effort, you can see what they are seeing and think what they are thinking. That, to me, is love.

Now, on the other side of the spectrum, there are lots of emotions that people confuse with love. One of the most common is attraction. There is a difference between being attracted to someone and wanting to spend the rest of your life with someone.

Some people fall into the trap of thinking they love someone just because they are afraid to be alone. They have become dependent on the other person for so much that they don't know how to make it on their own, or because they would much rather be with someone than no one.

This leads to the old cliché that in order to love another person, you must first learn to love yourself. Well, we've all heard that before, but what does it really mean? It means that you have to be confident in your own ability and your own judgement. You really have to like yourself and know what you have to offer another person. There is no way that you can love another person if you are so neurotic that you do anything they ask and agree with everything they say – just in case they won't like you any more if you don't behave like that.

Basically, the question of whether or not you are in love with someone is pretty obvious: you either are or you aren't … and, deep down, you know the answer. You just have to trust yourself to recognise it.

3 Look at the way the words and phrases in the box are used in the text on page 86, and then write them in the correct gaps below.

cliché

common

complicate

dependent on

fall into the trap

pretty obvious

harmony

judgement

neurotic

prospect

share

a People are in .... when they are peaceful and agree with each other.

b Someone who worries all the time is often called ....

c We often use the phrase .... to describe something that is clear and simple.

d When we expect something to happen we say that there is a .... of it happening.

e When someone makes a .... on something they decide what they think about it.

f A .... is a phrase that is repeated so often that we don't think about its meaning, such as 'blind as a bat' or 'raining buckets'.

g When something is normal and ordinary we can say that it is ....

h When two people .... something they experience it together.

i When we .... things we make them less clear and simple.

j When you always need the support of another person you are .... them.

k When someone offers you something for nothing, it's easy to .... of believing them.

. . . .

4 Is each of the following statements *True* or *False*? Write T or F in the brackets.

a Bob Narindra suggests that many people don't know whether what they are feeling is really love. [   ]

b He thinks that the love for a pet is the same as the love for a friend. [   ]

c He says that people who are in love want to tell the person they're in love with about everything that has happened to them. [   ]

d He thinks that people who are in love can read each other's minds. [   ]

e He suggests that you have to love others in order to be able to love yourself. [   ]

f He suggests that loving yourself means that you can make your own strong opinions. [   ]

g He warns that agreeing with anything the other person says is a sign of being too dependent on that person. [   ]

h He is sure how to answer the question 'Is this love?' [   ]

i I think Bob Narindra gives good advice! [   ]

●●● C 'Small ads'

1 **Good-looking** rock climber, 28, WLTM adventure-loving, athletic female for a lifetime of fun, the outdoor life and lots of parties. Box 555

2
Duty manager. Salary £260 per week. Experienced person needed for busy self-service restaurant in Gratten Centre. Applicant must be good with people and be responsible for good hygiene standards. 5-day week, daytime only. Call Steve for interview (01533

3 Harland Motors requires full-time qualified mechanic. Start immediately. Must be reliable and self-motivated. Good rate of pay for the right applicant. Tel: Sam or Adi on 01533

4 Female teacher, 40-something, loves classical music, theatre, art, seeks honest, gentle, sensitive, capable and amusing man for marriage. Box 329

5 **TELESALES** person required for fast-growing company. Experience preferred. Salary, hours negotiable. Call Ruth on 01293

1 Look at the newspaper advertisements (often called 'small ads'). Which one is looking for:

a ... someone to talk on the telephone all day?   [   ]
b ... a wife/girlfriend?   [   ]
c ... someone to work with cars?   [   ]
d ... a husband/boyfriend?   [   ]
e ... someone to work with food?   [   ]

Write the matching number in the brackets for each. ⚿

2 Match the words in the box with their meanings (a–i).

a friendly and polite:..

b keeping things clean:..

c walking, cycling etc.:..

d something that can be changed or agreed through discussion:
....

e someone who asks someone for a job:
....

f someone who fixes cars:..

g the money that is paid every month:..

h would like to meet:..

i the amount of money offered for a job: .... ⚿

applicant
hygiene
good with people
mechanic
negotiable
rate of pay
salary
the outdoor life
WLTM

3 Complete the following sentences using words from the advertisements.

a .... Mary on 01229 ...

b .... negotiable.

c 50-something man .... happy, artistic woman.

d Cook .... for new restaurant.

e Experience .... but not essential.

f The successful .... will earn a lot of money.

g The applicant must .... with people. ⚿

ANSWER KEY

UNIT 1

A 3
a relative
b enthusiastically
c attentively
d criticise
e inconvenient
f try your best

A 4
Example answers
1 Do you:
  a ignore the child.
  b ask the child what the problem is.
  c tell the child to be quiet.
2 Do you:
  a ignore the problem.
  b smile at the couple and say that you understand.
  c go over and tell them to be quiet.
3 Do you:
  a say 'It's my grandfather's book. I don't really want to lend it.'
  b lend it to your friend.
  c say no.

B 1
1 c
2 b
3 d
4 a
5 e
6 f

B 2
a Lensky
b Tatiana
c Lensky
d Madam Larina
e Onegin
f Ralph Fiennes
g Prince Gremin
h Onegin
i Tatiana and Onegin
j Tchaikovsky
k Pushkin
l Pushkin

B 3
a widow
b pours out their heart
c challenges someone to a duel
d can not walk away from
e in a strange mood
f passionately
g outgoing
h heartbroken
i landowner
j fictional
k ridiculous
l a twist of fate

C 1
a Sally
b John
c Justin

C 3
He is happy because he has just won the lottery.
Arran is a good football player although he is not very big.
Stephen is very excited because he has just won the lottery.
Stephen is very excited because of his lottery win.
He played a good game in spite of/despite feeling ill.
She missed the train in spite of /despite getting up early.
He is happy because of his lottery win.
Mark is not very popular despite/in spite of his friendly and enthusiastic manner.
He failed his exam despite/in spite of his hard work.
Sadia passed her exam although she is not very intelligent.

C 4
Example answers
Report 1: Andrew makes a lot of mistakes because he works too fast. Although he tries his best to make friends, he is not very popular because he tries too hard. He seems to be obsessed with music and he is sometimes careless.
Report 2: Andrew is a fast worker who tries his best to make friends. He is very creative. He is also very musical.

UNIT 2

A 1
a Some overalls.
b Lt Zachary Mayo.
c From the sea/from drowning.

A 2
Example answers
a Because he was hot and he couldn't sleep.
b He leaned too far over the side.
c He filled them with air and used them as a 'life jacket'.
d He hadn't seen anyone for 34 hours and he'd seen sharks.
e Two marines talked to Mayo's parents. Three days later they heard about his escape.

A 3
a press release
b the Pentagon
c stuffy
d bunk
e deck
f aircraft carrier
g ordeal
h miracle

A 4
a back to sleep
b thinking
c footing
d of madness
e consciousness
f his eyes

B 1
People who live in the house: Helen Monahan (————),
Marcus Monahan (boiler engineer),
Harley Monahan (————),
Norton Monahan (————)
Pilot: Donald Campbell (neurosurgeon)

B 2
a F
b T
c F
d F
e T
f T
g F

B 3
a pick up
b steer
c plunge
d grab
e treat
f clip
g plough through
h yaw
i cut out

B 4
a engine
b tail
c nose
d wing
e wing tip

C 1
a Fuel gauge failure traps couple
b Hero pulls neighbour from fire
c Horrified driver sees attack
d Saved by sharp-eyed flight attendant
e Turbulence terrifies teenager

C 2

a Articles (*the*, *a*), prepositions (*in*, *on*), auxiliary verbs (*is*, *are*, *have* etc.)

b Verbs, nouns, adjectives: dramatic words – the main events of the story

c The verbs are often written in the present simple tense.

C 3

a Turbulence terrifies teenager

b Horrified driver sees attack

c Saved by sharp-eyed flight attendant

d Hero pulls neighbour from fire

e Fuel gauge failure traps couple

C 4

a Gulay Menguç was terrified on a flight from Istanbul to New York by turbulence.

b Youths attacked a car with bricks and a baseball bat.

c Air hostess Julie saw a burning ship from an aeroplane.

d Jean Buiter was saved from a fire by her neighbour Laurence Broderick at her home.

e Jane Bakewell had forgotten her mobile phone so she and her husband had to spend the night in their car.

C 5

Example answers

a Worker nearly dies in freezer/Exercise saves locked-in worker

b Lorry smash kills 2/2 dead in motorway accident

c Warmheart concert cancelled/Illness stops Warmheart concert

d Teenager runs marathon for cancer research/15-year-old Emma runs for charity

UNIT 3

A 3

a F. The text says 'few shoppers go with lists', i.e. they haven't thought too carefully about what they want.

b T. The text says 'this makes them … feel positive'.

c F. The text says they are normally 'placed on the back wall'.

d F. The text says the middle shelves are considered the best.

e F. They must know. The text says that all supermarkets from one company choose the same colours.

f F. The text says that when people feel sleepy they buy more goods.

g T. The text says that fresh smells … 'create a nice "homely" feel'.

h F. The text says that silence makes people feel uncomfortable.

A 4

a aisle

b open-air

c carcasses

d vacuum-packed

e blink

f sell-by date

g background noise

h observe

A 5

Possible answers

This makes people think they are going into an open-air market …

… makes them feel positive, …

… colours that make people feel healthy and happy, …

… the same colours to make people feel at home, …

This can make customers feel sleepy, …

Silence makes shoppers feel uncomfortable …

A 6

There is some truth in both of these statements, but **a** is nearer the meaning of the text than **b**.

B 1

a 2

b 3

c 3

d 1

B 2

a site

b queue

c season

d madhouse

e exit ramps

f online

g hassle

h collide

i patrol

j creep along

k put things into perspective

l convenience

m shopping offline

n efficient

B 3

a 1 Arundel Mills Mall

2 $250 million

3 Baltimore, Maryland

4 7000

5 Shops, a movie theatre with 20 screens and an entertainment complex

6 Queues 'for miles'

b 1 People who have already used the Internet a lot

2 Small, only offering one thing, quick, easy to use, don't ask for personal information or go wrong

3 Customer focus, relevance, support, service, fulfilment

C 1

a They think that the Internet has changed the way people shop.

b It is possible to buy them on the Internet.

c They would still rather go to a shop.

d Computers have had an impact on the way they shop.

C 2

1 d

2 c

3 b

4 a

C 3

1 a

2 b

3 c

4 d

C 4

The correct order is: **c, b, d, a.**

UNIT 4

A 1

The correct answer is **b.**

A 2

a They are usually in their late teens or early twenties.

b They are students, secretaries, young lawyers, electricians.

c They are neither poor nor rich; they don't have too much money but they usually have enough to travel cheaply.

d Backpackerland exists because travelling is cheaper than ever before.

e By email.

A 3

a hostel

b air-conditioned

c jet-lagged

d cybercafés

e market stalls

f travel guides

g clamour

h bravest

A 4

1 hotter

2 the worst

3 more alive

4 more interesting-looking

5 cheaper

6 bravest

a the worst

b more alive

c bravest

d hotter

e more interesting-looking

f cheaper

A 5
a between (X and Y)
b completely at home
c cost the earth
d life is full of surprises
e out of touch

B 1
a F
b F
c F
d F
e T
f T
g T
h F
i T
j F

B 2
a bolt
b dozily
c chattering
d keep the flies at bay
e early-bird travellers
f die-hard party goers
g expectantly
h dawn chorus
i muffled
j clatters

B 3
a car horns, water pipes, Thai conversation
b bolts clicking open, the German girls' clogs
c a traveller who'd been in the same place the night before
d one of a group of Americans
e American: They're banana pancakes. They're the business.
Writer: They smell pretty good.
American: They taste better. Are you English?
Writer: Yes.
American: Have you been here long?
Writer: I've been here since yesterday evening. What about you?
American: I've been here for a week.

C 2
1 d
2 f
3 b
4 e
5 c
6 a

C 3
a A Scottish poet.
b Traditional Scottish sausage made of chopped meat and oats, boiled in a sheep's gut.
c A poem by Robert Burns.
d The Bishop of Ireland in the 5th century and a saint.
e A three-leafed clover.
f Good fun.

UNIT 5

A 1
a 4
b 1
c 6
d 5
e 3
f 2

A 2
a He's a writer.
b In a camper van.
c He thinks it's wonderful.

A 3
Example answers
a he lost his flat, he needed a new engine for his car and suddenly he found a van, which resolved both problems.
b he wasn't sure he could handle it (parking, washing, loneliness, life on the road, power for the computer).
c car parks, lay-bys, festival sites, by the roadside.
d it's great not knowing where you are, seeing new sights, beautiful scenery.
e using solar power.
f there's no rent, no obligations, a sense of freedom and happiness; the whole world is your home.

A 4
a An accident is something bad that happens when you don't expect it; accidental is when something happens that is not planned.
b A park is a large area of grass (often in a town) for relaxation; a car park is a special place for people to leave their cars.
c A site is a special place for something (a factory, town, festival etc.); a sight is something you see.
d A road sign is something that gives information about speed limits, directions etc; the roadside is the area at the side of a road.
e An optimist is someone who thinks that everything will be fine; a pessimist is someone who thinks everything that can go wrong will go wrong.
f A campsite is an area where people can put tents or mobile homes; a camper van is a van that has been adapted for people to live in.

A 5
a cope with
b spends a lot of time
c make a decision
d a sense of freedom
e has no doubt (that)

B 1
The verses are currently in the order 2, 1, 3.

B 2
a wearing
b poor
c nothing
d clothes
e clumsily
f patiently
g smirks
h inside

B 3
a I am completely different
b The confession
c The confession
d I am completely different
e I am completely different
f The confession
g The confession
h (You decide!)

C 1
a Flat 3, 156 Centenary Road, Mumbai, India.
b By bus.
c At first she was nervous, pessimistic; things have improved since then, so she's fine, though she still can't believe it.
d Brenda's a pessimist. Mariel's an optimist.
e Brenda's a teacher. Mariel works in films.
f David is probably Rosemary's husband.
g Although the layout is quite formal, the letter itself is very informal and friendly, with expressions like 'You know me', 'So the big news is, we've made our decision', and signing off with 'love'.

C 2
a I
b F
c N
d F
e F
f N
g I
h F
i F
j I
k N
l F
m I
n F

UNIT 6

A 1

Mary Read

a 1690–1720

b British

c She was disguised as a boy so that she coul inherit her grandmother's money. She fought and lived as a man.

d She fought in the British army. She married a soldier. She was captured by pirates. She fought as a pirate. She had a baby in prison.

e Jack Rackham & Anne Bonney, pirates; two soldiers

f She was imprisoned but not executed because she had a baby.

Cristina Sánchez

a 1972 ---

b Spanish

c She fought as a matador, usually a male occupation.

d She started bullfighting in South America in 1992. She was criticised. She retired in 1999.

e –

f She was fed up with criticism, so she retired.

Calamity Jane

a 1852–1903

b American

c She fought like a man (often dressed as a man) and was famous for her bravery.

d She fought with the US army in the 1870s. She saved a captain who fell from his horse. She met Wild Bill Hickock and went to live with him in Deadwood. She ran a ranch and an inn. She married and had a daughter.

e The captain who called her 'Calamity Jane'; Wild Bill Hickock; Clinton Burke (her husband)

f She tried to raise cattle and then ran an inn, but she was not successful.

A 2

a Mary Read

b Cristina Sánchez

c Calamity Jane

d Mary Read

e Calamity Jane

f Wild Bill Hickock

A 3

a on foot

b fell in love with

c the ban was lifted

d settled in, on horseback

e Much to my surprise

B 1

1 Catherine of Aragon

2 Anne Boleyn

3 Jane Seymour

4 Anne of Cleves

5 Catherine Howard

6 Catherine Parr

B 2

a male heir

b proof

c contemporary accounts

d control

e niece

f superb shot

g died in childbirth

h accomplished

i athletic

j good politics

k disastrous

l horseman

B 3

a sport, horse riding, archery, tennis, music

b 1 Mary
  2 Elizabeth
  3 Edward

c 1 Edward
  2 Mary
  3 Elizabeth

d Catherine of Aragon

e Jane Seymour

f Anne of Cleves

g Catherine of Aragon

C 1

Example answers

a What's your name?

b When were you born, and where were you born?

c Where are you from? Where do you live? Have you lived anywhere else? Where were you educated?

d What have been some of the important events in your life so far?

e What's the most important thing that has happened to you recently?

f How would you describe yourself?

g What are your interests?

h What do you hope for in the future?

UNIT 7

A 4

a quit smoking, join a gym, go on a diet, spend more time on housework, cut down on chocolate

b it's easier to say it than do it, our appetites return and we start to feel deprived, the results are not immediately visible

A 5

a can't cope

b a distant memory

c in control of

d nobody's perfect

e on a diet

f feel like

g gain satisfaction

h at risk

B 1

a Angela Jones

b Nigel Jones

c Ronald Crabtree

d Daisy Crabtree

B 2

a Angela and Nigel

b Thompson Cruises

c Angela

d Bishop Jonathan Blake

e Sasha Pliotnov

f Nigel and Angela

g My Travel Group

h The tour operator, Kuoni

i Roger and Daisy

j Daisy

B 3

a romantic setting

b the tip of an iceberg

c wedding package

d exotic location

e got to my level

f out of the ordinary

g in style

h wedding reception

i hand in hand

C 1

a Mr and Mrs Gurney's invitation to the wedding of their daughter.

b The e-mail invitation from Jed.

c 1 Old (Mr and Mrs Gurney must be old enough to have a grown-up daughter.)
  2 Young (Rosie is probably in her late teens/early twenties; the party is at a club; she uses language like 'the coolest party in town', which suggests she is a fairly young person.)
  3 Young (Carol, Gita, Sasha and Miguel probably share a house, so they might be late twenties/early thirties).
  4 Young (Jed is probably in his early twenties (or late teens); he uses text message language (e.g. CU, BTW), which is more common for that age group.)

C 2

a who's sending it; what kind of an event; time, date and place of the event

b '... have great pleasure in inviting you to ...'; 'Come and celebrate ...'; '... would like to invite you'; 'Any chance you can come to my party ...?'

c Reply (RSVP); bring a bottle; let us know if you can come; bring a bottle and something to eat

d 1 smile
  2 see you
  3 by the way

UNIT 8

A 1

a Paintings or tags on the side of buildings, bridges, buses and trains.
b The text suggests that most people don't like it and that graffiti artists are usually punished.

A 2

a A graffiti artist's signature.
b Two teenagers who were prosecuted in Newcastle for causing £30,000 damage to public buildings.
c Graffiti artist Simon Sunderland.
d Barnsley Council.
e 'Fisto' or 'Fista'.
f The local council spent £500,000 a year cleaning up graffiti.
g A man who saw him painting complained to him. Sunderland spray-painted the man.
h A policeman.

A 3

a signature
b invent
c penalties
d offences
e prosecuted
f sites
g spray-paint

A 5

a According to the police
b It gives me a buzz
c On one occasion
d went up to him
e things came to an end
f It soon became clear
g go to prison for a long time

B 1

Jean-Michel Basquiat
1960–1988
New York
Haitian father, Puerto Rican mother
Played in a band, doing graffiti, painting
All over America, Paris and New York
Basquiat
Jeffrey Wright, David Bowie, Courtney Love

B 2

a Jean-Michel Basquiat
b Thompkins Square Park
c Jean-Michel Basquiat
d Madonna
e Andy Warhol
f Jean-Michel Basquiat
g John Seed
h Julian Schnabel
i Julian Schnabel

B 3

a Syrup
b Image
c searching for some kind of identity
d quit school

e encourage your interest
f simultaneous
g stars
h at the height of their powers

C 1

a The dog chased the rabbit.
b Mr Jesperson owns the rabbit.
c Mr Jesperson bit the dog.
d Mrs Ramsey took down the fence.
e Harmony is Mr Jesperson's wife.
f Mrs Ramsey and Mr Jesperson are neighbours.

C 2

a The present simple.
b The headline misses out articles, auxiliaries and prepositions.
c 1 The first paragraph, tells the whole story briefly as an introduction.
  2 The second paragraph explains the first parts of the story in more detail.
  3 The next paragraph completes the story.
  4 The final paragraph concludes the article by looking to the future.
d They are possessive adjectives.
e The underlined words refer back to previously mentioned nouns/names, e.g. his = Mr Jesperson, her = Mrs Carol Ramsey, their = William Jesperson and Carol Ramsey.

UNIT 9

A 2

a crossing your arms
b scratching your head
c shrugging your shoulders
d smiling
e waving
f tapping your foot

A 3

a intimacy
b universal
c uncertain
d fidgeting
e strangers
f subconsciously
g protect yourself

A 4

a Because they are happy.
b Because they are surprised/interested.
c Because they are uncertain or worried.
d Because they don't know something or don't care.
e Because they are relaxed or bored, or want to protect themselves.
f To say hello or goodbye.
g To show they are puzzled.

A 5

face-to-face – without seeing the people we're talking to
out of place – appropriate
telling the truth – lying

A 6

a telling the truth
b face-to-face
c out of place

B 2

a 2
b 3
c 2
d 1
e 2

B 3

a T
b T
c T
d F
e F
f T
g F
h T
i T

B 4

a interviewer
b unconsciously
c relax
d uncrossed
e sit forward
f eager/enthusiastic
g lower
h the same
i enter
j decisive
k appropriate
l enrol

C 1

a A bank robbery.
b Three.

C 2

a The raid took place at about 1.30pm, not 12.30 as in the statement.
b The man with the gun had long grey hair, not short dark hair as in the witness statement.
c The second man was wearing a blue T-shirt, not a black sweater as in the witness statement.

C 3

Example answer
Policeman: What did you see?
Witness: Well I saw two men running away from a house.
Policeman: Were they carrying anything?
Witness: Yes. One of them was carrying a backpack, which seemed pretty full. The other one had two pictures with him. They'd obviously just taken them from the house.

Policeman: Can you describe the men?
Witness: Yes, of course. The first one –
the one with the backpack – was tall
and skinny. The other one – the one
with the pictures – was shorter and
quite fat. He was wearing a cap.
Policeman: Anything else?
Witness: Yes. A window of the house
was broken.

C 4
Example answer
WITNESS STATEMENT
I was walking along the street when I
saw two men walking down the street.
They had obviously just come from a
house. I could see a broken window in
the house.
One of the men was tall and skinny.
He had a large backpack, which
appeared to be full. The other man
was shorter and fatter. He was
wearing a cap. He was carrying two
pictures.

UNIT 10

A 3
a paragraph 3
b paragraph 1
c paragraph 10
d paragraph 7
e paragraph 2
f paragraph 4
g paragraph 9
h paragraph 12
i paragraph 8
j paragraph 6
k paragraph 5
l paragraph 11

A 5
a By the time
b not a good idea
c out of date
d long periods of
e raves about
f nothing wrong with that
g down the drain

B 1
a T
b F
c T
d F
e F
f F
g F
h T
i T
j F

B 2
a digital camera
b technically complex
c Internet service provider
d a small computer that you can
carry with you
e technically simple

f a 'place' on the Internet that you
can visit
g see you
h uniform resource locator (the
address of a website or web page)
i World Wide Web

B 3
a 55 minutes
b On the train
c 1 Laptop computer
2 Mobile phone
3 Digital camera
d 1 Sending emails
2 Design work
3 Computer games
4 Homework
5 Shopping
6 Booking holidays
e You can answer emails in your own
time.

C 1
a today
b all the best
c before eight
d be seeing you
e by the way
f see you later
g great
h lots of love
i love
j anyone
k no one
l Oh I see
m Are you OK?
n someone
o thanks
p want to
q weekend
r love and kisses

C 2
a Do you want to come out with me?
b Clown's café?
c Fantastic! See you tomorrow.
d Great.
e Oh please. Just once.
f Tomorrow? See you about eight?
g OK. See you then.
h No thanks.
i Where?
j When?
k OK. Just once.

1 a
2 h
3 e
4 k
5 d
6 i
7 b
8 j
9 f
10 g
11 c

UNIT 11

A 1
a William Shakespeare was born in
Stratford-upon-Avon.
b William Shakespeare wrote Romeo
and Juliet.
c Many films have been made about
William Shakespeare and his plays.
d Apparently William Shakespeare
wasn't educated enough for such a
knowledgeable playwright.
e There are no handwritten
manuscripts in William
Shakespeare's handwriting.
f Some people think the Earl of
Oxford used the name 'William
Shakespeare' but that he (the Earl
of Oxford) wrote the plays.

A 2
a T
b T
c F
d T
e F
f T

A 3
1 A
2 H
3 G
4 B
5 C
6 D
7 I
8 F
9 E

A 4
a John Field was Shakespeare's
neighbour in Stratford-upon-Avon
and he published books.
b William Shakespeare.
c In these texts there are two, one at
Stratford and one at Bilton.
d 1623.
e 1580.

B 1
a Margaret Johnson
b Alex Faye
c Brad Courtenay
d Ralph Blackman
e Brad Courtenay

B 2
a 2
b 4
c 5
d 6
e 3
f 1

B 3
a T
b T
c T
d T
e F
f F

g F
h F
i F
j T
k T

C 3
a 6
b 5
c 4
d 2
e 1
f 3

UNIT 12

A 1
The correct answer is c.

A 2
a 4
b 1
c 5
d 2
e 3

A 3
a Paul.
b Bob.
c Football.
d 1 He misses training sessions.
  2 He's unfit/out of shape.
  3 He's out at parties all the time.
e They are brothers.

A 4
a awkward
b stammer
c stretch
d hardly
e training sessions
f fashionable
g get up to
h stadium

A 5
a turned his back
b get into shape
c had enough of
d change your ways
e makes two of us
f interrupting
g read his thoughts

B 1
a Fulham LFC
b Stowmarket
c Chantelle White
d Permi Jhooti
e Permi Jhooti
f Rachel Yankey
g Two teenagers at Rachel's training session
h Clinton Joseph
i A middle-aged man

B 2
a damp
b professional
c role model
d look up to
e enthusiastic

f blokes
g ref
h side
i coordinator
j typical
k inspiring

B 3
a it is the only fully professional women's side in Britain
b she says she loves it and she's really lucky to be playing it
c there were no women footballer role models
d they were sending text messages
e they weren't laughing

C 1
R 4
I 3
C 1
E 2

C 2
a Pain tells you whether you need to see a doctor.
b Like ice, a bag of frozen peas can help to stop the swelling.
c You can wrap the bag of frozen peas in a towel.
d Heat is bad because it increases the swelling.
e A bandage helps to stop bleeding and reduce the swelling.
f You have to raise your leg above hip level within 24 hours.

C 3
a scuba
b laser
c NATO
d UNESCO
e VAT

UNIT 13

A 1
a Yo-Yo Ma, the cellist.
b 600.
c empty, dangerous, loud, painful – almost unbearable
d They held their breath – complete silence.
e Yo-Yo Ma beckoned to someone in the audience, went down to meet him and they embraced.
f They started cheering and shouting.

A 2
a music stand
  conductor
  cellist
  piano
b nervous
  excited
  emotional
c dangerous
  painful
  unbearable
  terrible
  dark

A 3
a moved about on the chair until he felt comfortable.
b not a single sound
c stopped breathing for a while
d embraced wildly
e applauded and cheered wildly

A 4
a You hold your breath.
b You make yourself comfortable.
c Complete silence.
d You'd fling your arms around each other.
e You might go crazy.

B 1
a They were waiting to buy bread.
b A mortar shell exploded in the street.
c 22.
d At four o'clock.
e They were innocent people – men, women and children.
f Vedran Smailovic was a 35-year-old man who lived nearby.

B 2
a He was a cellist with the Sarajevo opera.
b He decided to do something about it. He played his cello in the street.
c Albinoni's Adagio in G.
d He played for compassion and peace, to ease the pain of loss, and to preserve the dignity of the human race.
e No, he was never hurt.

B 3
a He is an English composer.
b He read about a man who played his cello in the street to honour the dead.
c He wrote a special piece of music called The Cellist of Sarajevo.
d At the Manchester cello festival.
e Yo-Yo Ma.
f Vedran Smailovic.

B 4
a The Cellist of Sarajevo.
b David Wilde.
c Because he had read about Vedran Smailovic.
d He had played his cello in the streets in order to honour the dead.
e Vedran Smailovic.

C 1
a ʎ
b [ ]
c sp
d ww
e g
f c
g p
h t
i wo

C 2
Example answer
Music is my favourite thing. I like it very much. I learned the piano when I was young but now I don't play very much at all.
My sister plays in a rock band. She is very keen on heavy metal music, though I don't like it at all because I prefer jazz-style music.
My friend Peter likes heavy metal music too. He has a lot of information about it – and he also likes my sister a lot!

C 4
For (in favour of) learning a musical instrument: a, b, c, h, i, j
Against learning a musical instrument: d, e, f, g, k, l

C 5
Example answers
In favour
Children should learn a musical instrument at school because music can be enjoyed all your life. But it's more than that. Children develop intellectually when they learn an instrument and they take pride in their progress. Playing music helps mind and body coordination, and playing in music groups is good for cooperation.
Against
Although music has some advantages, I don't think all children should learn a musical instrument at school. Some children are bored by music, and not all of them have musical talent. There is nothing special about music; other subjects such as maths and science are more important. Not only that, but musical instruments are expensive to buy.

UNIT 14

A1
The correct answer is **b**.

A 2
a fool
b blush
c crazy about
d react
e criticising
f cross
g snap

A 3
a He likes Rachel. He is a musician and wants a nice house and to travel. He is crazy about someone called Malgosia, and says that he didn't listen to Rachel properly.
b She is quiet and gentle, has light brown hair and pretty brown eyes set in a pleasant face, and is easy to talk to. She likes the narrator a lot, probably.
c He is someone Malgosia is crazy about, but Rachel doesn't like him.
d She is really beautiful. She is crazy about Tibor, but is probably not in love with the narrator – who thinks she is more than his friend.

A 4
a 'Can I say something?' Rachel asked, nervously.
b 'I know that, you fool,' she said, laughing at me.
c 'Well, what?' I answered.

A 5
a ... to talk to (there was no problem having a conversation with her)
b ... for you (that's not the girl you should be with)
c ... your time (nothing is going to happen however long you go on, however hard you try)
d ... you think (your opinion is not important to me)
e ... your business (I don't want you to have opinions about my events in my life)
f ... my affairs (don't get involved with my private life)
g ... too far (I had said too much/spoken too strongly)
Phrases **d** and **f** are used aggressively.

B 2
a 6
b 1
c 7
d 2
e 5
f 3
g 4
h 8
i 9

B 3
a harmony
b neurotic
c pretty obvious
d prospect
e judgement
f cliché
g common
h share
i complicate
j dependent on
k fall into the trap

B 4
a T
b F
c T
d T
e F
f F
g T
h F
i (You decide!)

C 1
a 5
b 1
c 3
d 4
e 2

C 2
a good with people
b hygiene
c the outdoor life
d negotiable
e applicant
f mechanic
g salary
h WLTM
i rate of pay

C 3
a Call/ring
b Salary/Rates of pay
c WLTM
d needed
e preferred
f applicant
g be good with